The Journey Not the Destination

The Journey Not the Destination

a memoir by

Edward Gerrish Mair

With Reverend David Thurber Mair

The Journey Not the Destination

ISBN-9781654123437

KESTREL HILL PRESS

Contents

Dedication

This book is dedicated to all my family and friends who have brought both joy and sorrow to my life. For such is life. I am especially grateful to all my fellow travelers in the various 12 Step programs I have attended.

I would especially like to remember some of my family and friends who have already passed way: Edward Baker, Granville Vernon Baum, Kathryn Conover Baum, Frances Crowe, Eileen Cummings, Milton Feder, Cynthia Fisk, Richard Gale, Bobby Gibson, Bill Goldman, Jim Hill, Joe Hogan, Nancy, Isaacs, Sandy Isaacs, Anne Keppler, Loretta Land, Evelyn Thurber Mair, Rev. David Thurber Mair, George Fisk Mair, Jean Baum Mair, Margaret Mair, Patricia Mair, Reverend George Mair, Jim McNalley, Richard Morin, Gary Mysorski, Kathleen Pierson, Peggy Rieber, Marcia Sczygial, Patsy Shotswell, William Taggart, Marty Tenerowitz, Donald M.D. Thurber, Gerrish Thurber, Steve Trudel, Annie Tunstall, and Greg Williams

Acknowledgements

For Betty Turner and Margy Powell who helped proofread this document and Bob Turner who made me many cups of coffee!

For the staffs of Newburyport Library Archival Center and Hampstead Library who welcomed me to spend many hours working on this book. And for the Board of Directors of the Sons and Daughters of the First Settlers of Newbury who got me started on writing again!

For my family including: Phoebe Arias, Pamela Fisk, Brian Fisk, Alex Mair Goss, Ashton Goss, Vera Goss, Brayden Goss, Steve Goss, Cindy Kaeble, Sarak Kowalczyk, Douglas Mair, Patric Mair, Kathy Powell, Logan Powell, Jackson Petroules, Jaden Petroules, Lana Petroules, Nick Petroules, Shaina Petroules, Bill Taggart, Diane King-Taggart, Barbara Taggart Hall,

For my longest term and closest friends including: Lila Abu-lughod, Ruth and Dale Albert, Amy Weinberg, Sam & Joan Baily, Rich Beattie, Bill Belliveau, Howie Bond, Jane Czech, Saul Chadis, Peter Clark, Kathy Cymbura, Dr. Thomas Crowe, Susan Duffy, Jason Eisack, Bob Evans and Peg McIntosh, Katy Gibbs, Bill and Patricia Hermon, Chris Hughes, Karen Emel, John Keppler, Peter Land, Dan Linehan, Fred Oulette, Sarah Poole, Mary Ann Puter, Cathi Ross, David Ross, Elena Smalky, Warren Sanford, and Vinette Varvaro

For my former wives: Betsy Edna Thomas, Deidre Sousa, and Jane Lesley.

For my pets: Angus, Gandhi, Sarah, Erica, Athena. Nickels, Sneakers, Maisy, Chelsea, Chloe, Argo, and Venus

And most of all for my life partner: Margy Moss Powell

Table of Contents

Contents

TABLE OF FIGURES

Contents

Contents

Forward

This book is based upon a correspondence I had with my uncle, the Reverend David Thurber Mair, my father's brother. Uncle David was a Presbyterian Minister that served churches in Cortland, New York, Marietta, Ohio, Maryville, Tennessee, Hanover, Indiana, Detroit and Marquette, Michigan. He lived a long productive life, as did his wife Patricia. When I was a child, we visited with Uncle David and Aunt Pat in Maryville, Tennessee, Detroit, Michigan, and California where my Uncle was getting his S.T.D. degree and my father was teaching at UC Berkeley. My sister Marggie and I visited them three times in Marquette, MI before they died. I believe Marggie had also visited them at other times before. Uncle David and my sister Marggie both died in 2015. In 2015, I spent Christmas with my cousin Patric Mair, and Aunt Pat Mair who died in 2018.

Most biographies are written by or about famous and powerful people. I do not consider myself either. I realize that I am a privileged white male who had opportunities that may not have been available to others, but I am an average, privileged white male living in the 20th and 21st century and that may be of interest to some future historian, descendant, or thesis writer.

I do not expect my life is any more thrilling than most people's lives are, but it is my life so I thought I would record it as best I can. My life became more peaceful after I quit drinking in 1985 although my life may have not been as worldly successful since then.

Writing this book and seeking permission to use photographs has been an interesting process. Most people said yes, a few said no, a few I couldn't find. I took most of the photos myself and include only those of people who have given me permission.

Going back 40 or 50 years does stir up memories forgotten! In a few cases I have substituted pictures from my 2001 trip to Scotland and my 2006 trip to England, the island of my ancestors, for pictures I could not get permission to use. These trips were very meaningful to me. These pictures may appear to be out of place!

Joseph Campbell said, "follow your passion." Elizabeth Gilbert said," follow your curiosity." In my life, I have found that curiosity often leads to passion. My heroes include Mahatma Gandhi, Henry David Thoreau, Bill Wilson, and Mary Ann Rolfe. My passions are Quakerism, bird watching, the twelve steps, and genealogy.

In these pages, I record my feelings and facts as I remember them. If others disagree with my memories, I apologize in advance. My memory is no better than any other person's memory and my perceptions may differ from other persons' perceptions. I ask that readers remember that I will happily remove or replace any picture or text upon written request to Marshhawk@aol.com. E. Mair 12/30/2019

Figure 1 Edward Gerrish Mair Growing Up

Figure 2 Rev. Edward Gerrish Thurber siblings

Introduction

Let us begin when Bertha met Sam in Paris in the 19th Century. Bertha Fisk (1874-1958) met Samuel Wood Thurber (1867-1926) in Paris, France where his father, Rev. Edward Gerrish Thurber (1836-1913), was pastor of the American Church. Rev. Thurber and his wife Sarah Augusta Wood (1840-1914) eventually returned to Syracuse, NY. Rev. Edward's father, Jefferson Gage Thurber (1807-1857), died young in Michigan where he was Speaker of the Michigan Legislature.

Jefferson's wife, Mary Bartlett Gerrish Thurber (1815-1884), after Jefferson's death, married second, her son's wife's father Samuel Wood (1807-1889). Yes, she really did. In addition, her parents were first cousins Betsy Gerrish (1787-1821) and Thomas Gerrish (1786-1875). Samuel Wood's first wife, the mother of Sarah Augusta Wood (1840-1914), had died. Her name was Lydia Gerrish (1816-1866).

Samuel Wood's mother was Sarah.... you guessed it.... Gerrish (1766-1834). Therefore, I have five Gerrish lines going back to the original immigrant William Gerrish (1617-1687). He arrived in Newbury, MA in 1639. It is also why the Gerrish family has been of interest to me in my genealogical research. The Gerrish connection is why several of our family have the name Gerrish as part of our name!

Biographical Sketch
of the
Reverend Edward G. Thurber, D.D.

Read at the Presbytery of New York,

A long and most useful life ended in New York City, November 7, 1913, when the Rev. Edward G. Thurber, D. D., was suddenly called to the higher service of the same Master he had served so well here. Without pain, and with no "sadness of fare-

Figure 3 Rev. Edward Gerrish Thurber Sermon Cover

Bertha Fisk and Dr. Samuel Thurber had three children, my grandmother, Evelyn Thurber Mair (1898-1989), Louise (1900-1968), and Gerrish (1907-2000). Most of our family whom I have known are descended from one of these three children.

Figure 5 Jefferson Gage Thurber

Figure 4 Bertha Fisk Thurber

Evelyn Thurber married my grandfather, Rev. George Mair (1885-1962), who emigrated from Scotland and attended Mt. Hermon School, Wesleyan College, Harvard University and Union

Figure 6 Sarah Augusta Wood

Figure 7 Elizabeth Mair

Figure 8 Louise, Evelyn, and Bertha Thurber

Figure 9 Named after Bertha Fisk and her brother Wilbur

Theological Seminary, all of which he paid for himself through working summers in a New Hampshire granite quarry. Louise married William Taggart (a banker). Gerrish married Mary Zweizig and later, after Mary died, Jeanette Webster. Gerrish and Jeanette were married at Princeton Hospital where Gerrish was a patient.

Figure 10 Samuel Wood and Mary Bartlett Gerrish and Children

Evelyn Thurber and Rev. George Mair also had three children. Their daughter Betty (1923-1945) died quite young, Uncle David recalls his sister as someone with a gentle and pleasing personality. I have realized lately that my grandmother Evelyn lost most of her family before she herself died in 1989. She lost Betty in 1945, her husband George Mair in 1962 and my father George Fisk Mair in 1978.

The Journey Not the Destination

My parents George Fisk Mair and Jean Lois Baum (1919-2010) were married Dec 27, 1947 in a snowstorm in Princeton, NJ. My grandfather Rev. George Mair performed the marriage and my uncle Rev. David Thurber Mair was best man.

In my ancestry there are several Protestant ministers. My childhood included Sunday school and Church. I left the Church in 4th grade and didn't return until 1995. I didn't really become comfortable with the trinity until 2019. Today I am a Quaker and Believer and not ashamed of being so.

Figure 11 Kathryn Conover Baum

Figure 10 Elise Van Note and J. Fred Conover

My Mother's Family – Jean Lois Baum Mair (1919-2010)

Most of my mother's family were originally Dutch having settled in Manhattan (New Amsterdam) and Brooklyn (New Town) in the 1600s. The names include Van Kouwenhoven and Van Note. There is also a smattering of English families who settled in Monmouth County, New Jersey. Of interest to me were the Quaker families who migrated from Rhode Island to New Jersey. These include the Bordens and Claytons. My mother described her great grandmother, Rachel Borden (1848-1937) as a "peculiar women" who always wore a bonnet. The Clayton family can be traced back to Swarthmore Hall in England where Richard Clayton (1601-1625) was a servant of George Fox the Quaker Founder and a member of the founding Quakers (The Valiant 60). His sister Anne married two Governors of Rhode Island. My cousin Joan Potts Michealree has done considerable research on these families. The Van Kouwenhoven name morphed into Covenhoven and finally Conover.

Figure 12 Granville Vernon Baum

Granville Vernon Baum, my mother's father, who was born in Norfolk, VA and died in New Jersey. When I was a child we often attended Baum family reunions in Virginia and North Carolina. There are two books about this family by Elizabeth Baum Hanbury. Currituck Legacy is a genealogy. Getting to Pine Island is a fictional history.

The Van Notes (Dutch Reformed) and Claytons (Quakers)

Figure 13 Van Notes and Claytons

Chapter I – New Jersey 1951-1953. 1956.

Figure 14 Annie Tunstall and Richard Gale on our return from England in May 2006

My life began at the hospital in Princeton, New Jersey (March 20, 1951) and my burial will be at the Ewing Presbyterian Church Cemetery in New Jersey in the Fisk family plot which already contains the graves of my great great grandparents, great grandparents, grandparents, parents, and sister as well as others mentioned in this book.

I was born March 20, 1951 and my sister Marggie was born January 24, 1953. Our father who had been an Assistant Professor at Princeton University, moved to Smith College in 1953 and the family moved with him to 142 Green Street in Northampton, MA. Our father returned to Princeton in 1956 and in the summer of 1957 to complete work on his Ph.D. We lived in "The Project" on Harrison Avenue and I attended kindergarten in Princeton at the brand-new Little Brook School, 1956 is really the first year I have distinct memories of. We spent the summer of 1957 living in Princeton at

Professor Strayer's house on Prospect Avenue near the old alumni stadium.

My early memories include the smell of fresh tar, crab apple fights with other kids, being terrified of the alphabet in kindergarten, the death of a pet turtle, and being chased and kissed by the girls in my kindergarten class.

One of my friends in the Project was proud that his father was in the air force. Trying to one up him, I said that my father was a policeman and my mother was from India. Neither, of course was true. My father was on sabbatical from Smith College working at the Population Institute at Princeton and my mother was busy taking my sister to pre-school and me to kindergarten.

Figure 15 Fisk Family Plot in Ewing, NJ

My lifelong friend John Keppler was born at Princeton, NJ hospital the same year as I. We later became teenage friends in Northampton, Massachusetts and remain in touch to this day.

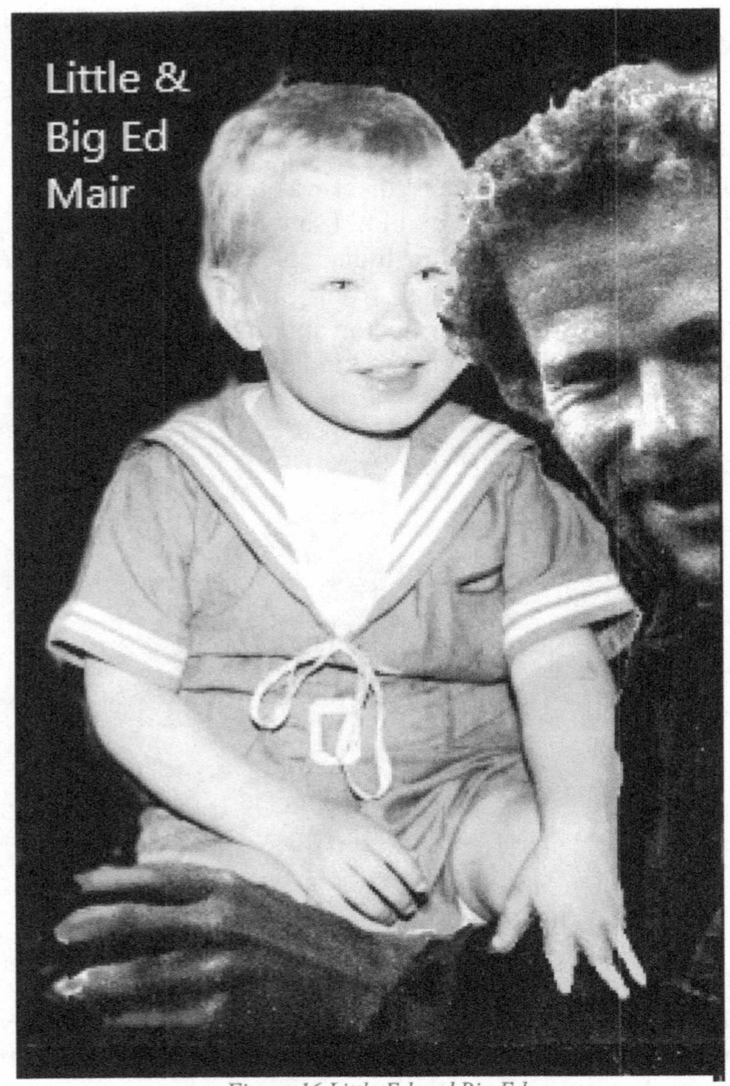

Figure 16 Little Ed and Big Ed

Chapter II Massachusetts 1953 -1960

Traumatic experiences from the 1950's

Figure 17 City Hall in Northampton, MA

These represent psychic wounds which I think I have now recovered from. However, I am sure they effected my decisions when I was a child and young adult.

Green Street neighborhood kids used to hang out at Paradise Pond on the Smith Campus in Northampton, MA. In the summer, as faculty children we could take canoes out from the boathouse and paddle up the Mill River. These were expeditions that I enjoyed. In the winter the pond was plowed, and sometimes when the snow was light, one could skate up the Mill River. I greatly enjoyed this too.

However, Paradise Pond on the Mill River was also the scene of a couple of unpleasant experiences for me! Once, when I was quite young, I fell through a hole in the ice. My young friends just stood around the hole laughing as I flailed around in the water in my water-logged snow suit. I was rescued by "Benny" the policeman who carried me home to Green Street soaking wet. I probably wasn't in the water very long, but it seemed like an eternity.

Another time, I was at Paradise Pond alone. The only other people there were a Smith College girl and her boyfriend. I was feeling how nice it was for them to be there together. Then they started arguing and pushing each other. I felt great sadness seeing this and I resolved in my young mind not to allow myself to have any such strong feelings in the future. And I don't think I did until I got sober in 1985!

While we were living on Green Street (which was from 1953 - 1959) we use to have babysitters who were Smith College girls. One sexually molested me. I remember she asked me to play a fun game and look up her tunnel with my flashlight. I said I didn't want to. She said I had too. I ran away and hid under the kitchen sink until my parents came home. She stormed around the house yelling that I was a very bad boy and that I should come out. My parents were told I was a bad boy. I couldn't really explain myself I remember. A few days later, the babysitter showed up with toy firehouse and fire engine as a gift to make peace, I guess. My parents thought it a lovely gesture. I stomped on the firehouse. That is really all I remember. I did discuss the incident with my mother when she was in her 70's and she didn't remember any of this. She thought it was a dream. I think it was real.

Bertha Fisk Thurber died in 1958 and my kindergarten best friend Bobby Gibson died in 1960. I remember saying over and over “it isn’t fair!” I had no idea at the time that these things are part of everyone’s life. These are the first deaths of people that I knew that I remember. My grandfather officiated at Bobby's funeral I have just learned from reading my grandfather's diaries.

We moved from 142 Green Street to 57 Washington Avenue in Northampton in 1959. My first-grade teacher was Mrs. Shortlidge and she had an Airedale dog named Bobbie that came to class with her. My second-grade teacher was Mrs. Meunier and my third-grade teacher was Mrs. Koester. In first grade I (and most of the other boys in the class) were in love with a third grader named Lisa. We would build castles out for blocks for her and then knock each other's castles down! Some things never change!

My mother sometimes became very angry and threw things around the house. One morning my sister and I hid under a bed to protect ourselves. I then went to second grade and reported during our "news" session what had happened. I remember the teacher scolded me and told the whole class that was not the type of news to bring.

Figure 18 First Family Car 1951 Plymouth

1960 - 1961

I was in a combined fourth grade-fifth grade with Mr. Fenn as the teacher. He and a twin brother had a summer home in Petersham, MA. The fifth grade gave him a new bicycle and I remember there was a huge controversy among parents as to whether he could accept it or not. That summer we visited the World's Fair in NYC. I remember Belgian Waffles were a big deal and I talked via video-link with a girl at the Chicago Museum of Science. This was the first year (at the World's Fair) where one could

Figure 19 Cottage at Eastham, MA Cape Cod

hear "It's a small world after all" which later became an attraction at Disneyland and one of those songs you can't get out of your head!

This may also have been the first year that we vacationed in Eastham, on Cape Cod, at "Dorothy's Cottage." This is one of my fondest memories of childhood. We spent two weeks each summer for several years here. The cottage had no electricity, heat, or plumbing. There was a pump in the kitchen, and we used kerosene lamps at night. There was an outhouse and the cottage perched on a dune overlooking the ocean at Coast Guard beach in Eastham. This was the place I was first introduced to biting green head flies, which you never forget once you have met them. Ironically, they are a regular, but brief, feature in July on Plum Island where I now live.

When I was older, I enjoyed surfing at Coast Guard beach in Eastham, Ma and Marconi beach in Wellfleet, MA. This is where I first drove a car and smoked a cigarette.

Figure 20 Bedford Park Presbyterian Church Bronx, NY

Chapter III – New York 1961 -1962

Figure 21 Christmas Cards from the Sixties

My family moved for the year to 107 Casillas Avenue in Yonkers on the edge of Bronxville. I was in fifth grade and both Marggie and I attended P.S. number 8 in Yonkers. My father was on sabbatical from Smith College and commuted to work in NYC at the Population Council. I remember he visited Jamaica, studied Russian, and was somehow involved with Planned Parenthood and the Rockefeller Foundation. I was in a bowling league winning my first and only trophy since our team finished second. I collected baseball cards, attended baseball games with my father, both the Yankees and Mets (who were in their first season). I remember seeing both Don Drysdale and Sandy Koufax pitch for the Dodgers against the Mets. I think this was also the year that Roger Maris and Mickey Mantle had a two-person home run derby.

This was the first year I was given peer information about sex, which

Figure 22 107 Casillas Ave. in Yonkers, NY

as it turned out was rather inaccurate. It was the first year I played

Figure 23 Rev. George Mair
b. Scotland 1885

spin the bottle and went to boy-girl parties. We visited Princeton and New York City often. We went to the television show College Bowl when Princeton University was on the show. We also attended the first productions of Sound of Music and My Fair Lady on Broadway and visited several museums including the Guggenheim Museum of Modern Art.

I was fascinated by the Mercury Astronauts this year and remember watching John Glenn's orbital trip in the gym of P.S. number 8 in Yonkers, NY.

The first time Marggie and I met our cousins Andy and Doug Mair was in Yonkers. Andy had a hard life and died in a car accident in Arizona in 1987 (See my Uncle David's notes later about this). Doug also had a hard life but now seems happy living in Indiana. My grandfather, Rev. George Mair died at age 75 of a brain tumor in Princeton, NJ this year and my mother had a "nervous breakdown."

My grandfather was a good man, but as a strict Calvinist, he had little use for Catholics, Jews, or fundamentalist Christians. My own moral struggles began then when I stole a transistor radio I found on the sidewalk and felt guilty about it. I kept it though!

Leslie Gore was from nearby Bronxville and I began to listen to popular music and baseball games under the covers at night on my "secret" radio.

The Reverend George Mair (1885-1961)

George Mair was born in 1885 in Aberdeen Scotland to Arthur Macdonald Mair (1850-1932) and Grace Anderson (1858-1938). Their parents were George Mair (1813-1912) Susan Simpson (1821-1856), Aneas Anderson (1830-1899) and Sophia Sheed (1836-1911).

The Mairs and the Andersons were tombstone makers. Sophia Sheed's brother Francis (1832-1918) immigrated to Australia.

This Francis Sheed had a grandson, also named Francis Sheed (1897-1981) who married Mary "Maisie" Ward (1889-1975) and they had a son named Wilfred Sheed (1930-2011). Wilfred Sheed was quite a well know author. One of his books, Frank and Masie, is about his parents whom I met as a child the year we lived in New York. My family had lunch with them in Scarsdale, NY. Frank and Maisie owned a Catholic Publishing House, which published in both New York and London. They were soapbox speakers in Hyde Park in London. Maisie was an expert on Elizabeth Barrett Browning. They are among the most interesting people I have met.

George Mair immigrated to America around the turn of the century and put himself through both Mt. Hermon School and Harvard University while working in granite quarries in the summer. He graduated from Harvard in 1916 and attended seminary school at Union Theological Seminary in New York, which he remained engaged with most of his life. He became a minister at Bedford Park Presbyterian Church in the Bronx, NY.

His immediate predecessor was William Sloan Coffin, Senior. Rev. Mair eventually became the head of the Presbytery of New York City. He was friends with Reinhold Niehbor who wrote the Serenity Prayer and Bill Wilson who was one of the founders of Alcoholics Anonymous. Things that I remember about my grandfather are his love of Robert Burns and that He had a workshop in his basement and would make my sister and me wooden toys there. When he retired, he and my grandmother Evelyn Thurber Mair moved to Princeton, NJ where he worked part time as a visiting Minister for The First Presbyterian Church on the edge of the Princeton University Campus. Both my father and I made pilgrimages to Scotland on our 50th birthdays.

Figure 24 Mair Family Photos from 50s and 60s

Rev. David Thurber Mair, Evelyn Mair, George Fisk Mair and the Mair families in Maryville, Tennessee 1960.

George Mair, Ed Mair, Marggie Mair, and Evelyn Thurber Mair around 1955.

Figure 25 Grace Anderson with son, later Rev. George Mair

George Mair (1813-1912) Udney, Scotland

Figure 26 George Mair grandfather of Rev. George Mair

Figure 27 Bob Elkins, Tom Crowe, and Ed Mair at Howie Bond's Bar Mitzvah

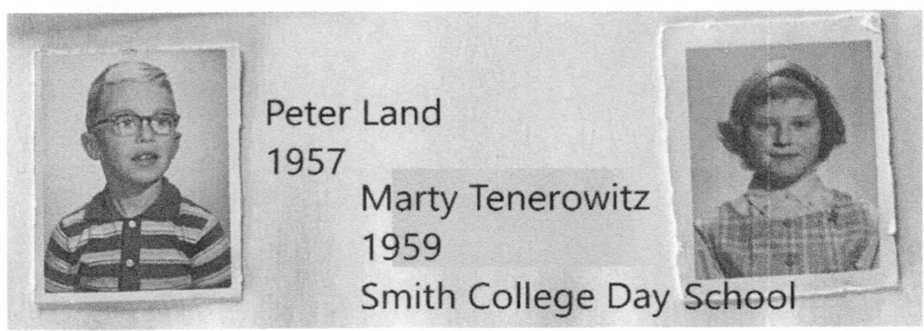

Figure 28 School Days 1950s

Upon returning to Northampton, from my father's sabbatical in New York, I spent a week in the Springfield hospital. I had a benign cyst in my upper jaw that was causing three adult teeth to come in upside down. A surgeon removed the cyst and teeth and I have had false teeth since then! I enjoyed the attention of my parents and friends and was not aware of the worry this situation must have caused my parents. For several months, my father took me frequently to follow up visits in downtown Springfield.

I learned the lesson of victimhood then. I played this card for attention later when I had the mumps, the measles, pneumonia and a broken leg. I learned as an adult that this ruse does not work when you are a smoker, an alcoholic, or have cancer. People have their own lives and their own problems. Poor me may work for kids but it becomes quite obnoxious in adults!

Music became increasingly significant in my life as I grew older. The first 45 records I bought were "Sugar Shack" by Jimmy Gilmore and the Fireballs and "I Want to Hold Your Hand" by the Beatles. We were not the greatest generation, but we did get to experience, the Beatles invasion, Woodstock, and Flower Power.

I recall attending a Jimmy Cliff reggae concert at the Academy of Music in Northampton. The whole theater was filled with marijuana smoke! At other times in my life I liked the Motown Sound and later country music. I attended several classical music concerts with my family, but I never really got hooked on this type of music. I appreciate the skill involved in playing Jazz. The soundtrack of my life, however, is rock and roll and rhythm and blues music.

When I was going through puberty and my voice was cracking, my music teacher told me not to sing because I was making everybody else sound bad. I have not sung since in public, although I think I have a good voice and would enjoy singing. This has become a lifelong trauma!

Chapter IV Northampton 1962 – 1964

I attended the Smith College Day School (SCDS) through 8th grade with the exception of fifth grade when we lived in New York. Many of my friends were faculty children at Smith College and I believe the school was a teaching and experimental school for the college. In any event, we learned "the new math" and so on. I studied both French and Latin. My sixth-grade teacher was Mrs. Arnold and my seventh-grade teacher was Mr. Hoyt. Mrs. Arnold was an English teacher and the mother of a friend of mine John Arnold. Mr. Hoyt had been the Massachusetts State Ornithologist and introduced me to bird watching. Actually, Mr. Hoyt took several of us on weekend excursions to the Mill River, Connecticut River, etc. You could not do that today I imagine but we had a grand time and I became a bird watcher for life!

These were the years I modified my bike with monkey handlebars and a banana seat. My father thought this preposterous! He pointed out that bikes had been evolving for comfort for 100 years and the standard design was probably the best. He was probably right, but the standard design wasn't cool was it?

I went to boy-girl dance parties, but I did not have a girlfriend. I am not sure if the Beatles arrived in 1963 or 1964. I do remember a debate with Chapin about whether the Beatles would last. Chapin said they were just a passing fad. Chapin and I were interested in the same girl, Marty.

Well, I won the girl sort of and the Beatles lasted! Marty held my hand in a tearful farewell the next year before I moved to Berkeley, CA for a year. In eleventh grade, Marty invited me to her junior prom at the Elms in Springfield, MA. Some years later, she moved next door to my mother and tragically died of a drug overdose. I still think of her from time to time.

October 1962 was the Cuban Missile Crisis and I remember we were all frightened at the time.

I had a season pass to ski at Mt. Tom in Holyoke, MA at night. We (friends my age) went three or four nights a week. This must have been hard on our parents, but we were totally addicted to the skiing. Probably in 1963, I broke my leg skiing at Stratton Mountain in Vermont with Robert. I spent the rest of the school year on crutches and my interest in skiing waned somewhat. The ride down the mountain with the ski patrol was quite painful!

In the summer, we played capture the flag on the lawn in front of the Davis Center at Smith College every night. This was a good time. I remember these years fondly. One activity of "the boys" was to build model cars and then load them with firecrackers and glue and go down by the Mill River to blow them up! I guess this was better than blowing up frogs.

I also went to Arcadia Day Camp, which was run by the Mass Audubon Society, and to the YMCA Camp. I really took an interest in nature at this time. Paul, Nancy, Robert, Howie, and I started the Monarch Antomology Club. The name was a devious suggestion on my part since my nickname was MAC and the correct word was Entomology. Nevertheless, the others bought it and I became president of the MAC club. We would go insect collecting and then come home and quite scientifically kill and mount the insects. We had the proper chemicals and equipment for this hobby, and we put together quite a good collection as I recall. I do remember having some problem with the killing part and I did let some pretty butterflies recover and fly away.

I really developed a fondness for the Mill River playing there a lot with friends and bird watching by myself. My first attempts at photography were there as well. On the far bank of the river was the Northampton State Hospital.

LBJ

I must go back a bit to 1960. I remember that I was selected to make a presentation to the whole Smith College Day School on Lyndon Baines Johnson when he ran for VP with JFK. There was one speaker on each candidate for VP (Henry Cabot Lodge was the GOP candidate for VP with Nixon). It is funny, LBJ is very well known now as a successful domestic President, an unsuccessful foreign policy President, and a master politician. Hardly anyone in Northampton knew who he was back then. It was probably my first research effort and I learned a lot and gave a good speech! Nobody in my circle knew much about Johnson at that time.

1963 was the year John F. Kennedy died. I was in a biology class dissecting a cat when the news flash came on the radio. I remember we had to finish what we were doing, clean up, and then we were sent home. Everyone, children and parents were in shock. Then I had a cold and so I was home sick watching live TV when Jack Ruby shot Lee Harvey Oswald. This is a very strong memory too.

1963 was the year we slipped into the Viet Nam war and the Beatles and the British invaded. This was a golden age of music for teenagers and I still remember the words to many Beatles songs.

In 1964, LBJ and Hubert Horatio Humphrey (HHH) ran against Barry Goldwater and Henry Cabot Lodge. I was an active LBJ supporter. At this time, I really got involved in politics, campaigning for whomever I liked. I guess it was cute. Anyway, at age 13 I got Christmas cards from several political leaders including Massachusetts governor Endicott "Chub" Peabody. I also started arguing with adults in the Letters to the Editor column of the local paper. I think my parents and their friends found this quite amusing!

In the summer of 1964, I spent a week with a friend Judson and his family in Camden, Maine. We sailed to Mohegan Island with the President of Bowdoin College, ate at the Camden yacht club and fished for dog sharks. What I remember most though was that Judson had a neighbor there (our age) who was as strong a supporter of Barry Goldwater as I was of Johnson and we argued constantly!

Figure 29 Port Clyde, ME 1964

Figure 30 Ed Mair at LBJ Rally 1964

These were also the years our family spent some time at Three Mile Island in Lake Winnipesaukee in New Hampshire at an Appalachian Mountain Club (AMC) camp. I remember this as an exciting time of new friends, sailing sunfish, canoeing on the lake and playing the guitar. Marggie did not have such such a good time there because I ignored her. Older brothers can be cruel!

I was in eighth grade at SCDS and our homeroom teacher was Mr. DeBaun. My class went through a "Jacks" fad, a game played with a ball and ten Jacks (small metal things with about six arms) I also used to have "wars" with Mike and David. We played elaborate war games with toy soldiers and fake guns on the Clark School property behind Crescent Street in Northampton. I suppose these were also the years that I was in cub scouts and then boy scouts. I was eventually patrol leader of the Bat Patrol and we won some sort of scouting contest at the Three County Fairgrounds Jamboree one year. We also took a 20-mile hike to Chesterfield, MA and went camping by ourselves a few times. The freedom kids had then, with hindsight, was wonderful!

Rev. David Thurber Mair adds:

I think everyone remembers where he or she were when John F. Kennedy was shot. I was then in Maryville, TN, and on that day was visiting a church member in his office (I think it was the county social services department) and we were trying to figure out how to help the Boy Scout troop in our church. Then the shocking news came, and we could not concentrate on what we had been doing. Therefore, we called it a day and I returned home. A sad pall hung over all of us. A retired minister in our congregation was scheduled to deliver the sermon that following Sunday on Stewardship (the pledge drive was about to begin) and the Session (official board of the church) decided to go ahead with that plan. During his sermon, I noticed nobody was listening; everyone's mind was on that national crisis. We should have switched gears and used that Sunday worship to reflect on what had happened in terms of our faith. We, too, were watching T.V. when Oswald was shot.

I have written a book about Andy Mair (unpublished). I have completed a second book – (also unpublished) - about my and Pat's civil rights involvements when I pastored in Tennessee. [The KKK burned a cross on Uncle David's lawn after he integrated his church Dave and Pat's children were Andy Mair, Doug Mair, and Patric Mair. -ed.]

Joshua Mair, Doug's son, is married to Chastity, has children and is located in Madison, Indiana. Madison is the county seat, a short distance from Hanover where I was pastor for 12 years. Andy and Doug both lived near their parents until Andy moved to an assisted living facility in Louisville, KY, 40 miles southwest of Hanover and across the Ohio River. Doug was here and there, living with Andy for a time as one of his caregivers, living with Kim, his son's mother, plus hanging out with friends.

Hanover is the home of Presbyterian-related Hanover College. The church building where I was pastor was the original college building until, in the middle 1800s, the college moved a few blocks away and established a beautiful campus on a bluff overlooking the Ohio River. The original building was altered with a peaked roof and sanctuary beneath it when a Presbyterian congregation was founded and occupied the building. When it was the college, building a theological seminary occupied a wing on the east side of the structure. The seminary eventually moved to a location in New Albany, IN, across the river from Louisville and later moved to Chicago when the McCormick family offered its money to the seminary which then became (and still is) McCormick Theological Seminary. The seminary wing in Hanover was torn down before the building was converted into a church. Today there is a large rock with a plaque on it, which occupies the spot where the seminary once existed, calling attention to the place where McCormick Seminary had its beginning.

Your grandfather, George, attended Wesleyan University in Connecticut for his freshman year in college - then transferred to Harvard as a sophomore. It was the class of 1916 and his 25th reunion was quite a bash. We all went except my mother. I do not know why she did not go. Two things stand out regarding that reunion that lasted several days. There was free Pepsi everywhere because one of the members of '16 was a Pepsi executive. The other great memory was an evening at the Boston Pops with Arthur Fiedler. We were brought to Symphony Hall in buses with police motorcycle escort with sirens wailing. Concerning Pop's employment in a granite quarry, he had the same job in Aberdeen, Scotland, before coming to America. He did lettering for tombstones which is maybe why he had the best penmanship in our family.

As I recall Uncle Bill was a banker [who was married to Louise Thurber, my mother Evelyn's sister. They had three children, Virginia, Joanne, and Bill. [All three of these children are also buried in the family plot in Ewing. Bill, Jr. was the father of my second cousins Cindy Taggart Kaeble, Diane, Barbara and Bill III who are twins. -ed]

Figure 31 Evelyn Thurber Mair relatives from Four Generations

My sister, Betty Mair, was plagued with ill health most of her young life. Scarlet fever and a disease called Puerperia - during surgery they found 2 and 1/2 spleens in her. She attended Oberlin College in Ohio for two years during which time she met her fiancé from Kentucky, Shelby. She came back home and attended a school (I draw a blank on what and where it was - maybe connected with Columbia Univ.?) where she studied Occupational Therapy, during which time T.B. of the spine was discovered. She entered a Manhattan hospital called Hospital for the Ruptured and Crippled to have her spine fused. Dr. Raymond Lewis took pictures of Betty's lungs, routine before surgery. Lo and behold he discovered the T.B. had spread to her lungs like a snowstorm! He and his wife, Alice, made a personal visit to my parents that evening with the news because Dr. Lewis knew Betty's case was terminal. The disease is called Milliary T.B. because it looks like tiny millet seeds. The disease crept up her neck into her brain; she became infantile in behavior and finally went into a coma. She died on my parent's 25th wedding anniversary. Yes, my mother suffered the loss of two children plus her husband before her death. I am so grateful I have lived beyond her death.

Andy Mair died on Dec. 12, 1987, on a highway west of Gallup, New Mexico. His girlfriend was following in her car. Andy was in his van adapted for the handicapped [Andy had been run over by a train earlier in his life and was in a wheelchair] and was pulling a trailer. They were hauling all their earthly possessions, hoping to settle in California (I think), but wanted, first, to travel to Hawaii. They had stopped in Gallup for supper and to get gas. Their habit was for him to follow her onto the freeway, then he would pull past her and then lead the way. After pulling in front of her, he hit black Ice (hard to see) and encountered strong winds. The van careened over to the right with the trailer fishtailing and crashed down an embankment. He was killed instantly. Robin stopped and waved for help. Months later Pat and I were in New Mexico for a Peace conference at a Presbyterian Conference Center, Ghost Ranch. We stayed with a friend in Albuquerque and drove to Gallup and talked with the state trooper who presided at the accident scene. He gave us good information.

I could write a book about Doug, also. He has come a long way from the life he led as a teenager. He pays close attention to us now and is very concerned about our welfare. On his visits here, he has done some amazing jobs for us around the house - I did not know how talented he is until those visits."

[Doug now lives in Madison, IN with his wife Jackie and near his brother Patric. -ed]

Pets and Wild Birds

I never bought a pet but adopted several, my childhood cat was named Angus and he was all gray as was a later pet cat named Nickle daughter of Sneakers. My closest companion was a cockapoo named Maisy. Maisy eventually moved to California and lived with Bob and Peg who had babysat for her during the day while I was at work. Maisy also lived with Bob and Peg for about a year in Madison, IN! At one time I had six cats.

Both Chloe and Chelsea who lived on Plum Island with Margy and me had to be put down after long lives with Margy as their primary caregiver. My dog Gandhi appears in the Chapter about San Francisco.

Of course, as an avid bird watcher, I have had feeders for many years and always enjoy my wild pets. In recent years, this has included a flock of about 11 turkeys that live in trees visible out the windows of our cottage on Plum Island. Plum Island is famous for its Snowy Owls in the winter. Newburyport is equally well known for Bald Eagles in the winter.

Plum Island is a wonderful place for a bird watcher to live.

Chapter V California 1964 – 1966

Figure 32 My first Airplane Ride in CA 1965

I find I reflect on my life in terms of what grade I was in or who my girlfriend was at the time, or what job I had. Of course, popular songs can trigger memories as well as certain smells like tar or diesel fuel or lavender. Anyway, my family spent about 12 months of time in California at this time while my father was on sabbatical at UC Berkeley. I was in 9th grade at Willard Junior High School. The Rolling Stones were big and the Beatles Revolver album was released this year.

Willard was a school that was probably 75% minority students. It had a tracking system though, and most of my daily classmates were white along with a few Asians. We only mixed with the lower tracks in athletics and at dances. I got in real hot water for a few days when I accused a black kid of stealing money from a white kid's locker (he did). For about a week I kept getting stares and threats of violence from many of the black kids in the school hallways. My dad made me keep going to school even though I was terrified. I guess he was right since nothing ever happened and that kid and I later became almost friendly. I don't know what other people's childhood experience was but when I look back it's almost as if I became friends with most of the kids, I had fights with. There was sort of a male butting heads type thing that eventually lead to mutual respect. This year stands out for me in many ways. One class I strangely remember liking was Latin. I joined the Student Patrol (hall monitors) later in the year.

Figure 33 Friends in Berkeley, CA 1965

This also happened to be the time that Ed Thurber [Ed Thurber is the son of Gerrish Thurber my grandmother Evelyn's brother -ed.] got married for the first time in Los Angeles. My family attended the wedding and the flight to Los Angeles on Pacific Southwest Airways was my first airplane trip. I loved and still enjoy flying! I have a mild fear of accidents, but it is not overwhelming.

I attended my first rock concerts this year, the Byrds and the Monkees (their first performance as a pilot before the TV Show aired). Some of the Viet Nam Day Committee protests occurred while we lived in Berkeley and I saw water hoses used on protesters. My father and I had a great time. I am not so sure that Marggie and my mother did. My dad enjoyed teaching at a large University, I think. I enjoyed surfing, working my way into the "in crowd" at the school, and generally just living in California. I got to surf at Half-Moon Bay and Malibu. I made several good friends that year and my school yearbook is full of warm goodbyes from several friends, male and female. My best friends as I recall were Marc B, David P, Kurt N, Ray G, Ken K and David C.

I wrote back home to Ruth about my adventures in California. She is a Judge today. I didn't really have a girlfriend this year, but I do remember dancing a lot with Ann, and remember Nancy, Debbie, Libby, and Molly as girls whose company I enjoyed. Four of these friends from 9th grade are Facebooks friends today (Libby, Ray, Will, and Ken.

My family drove back and forth from Massachusetts to California and stopped at many of the sites along the way. I first fell in love with the west on this trip visiting places like Yellowstone, Mt Rushmore, the Badlands, Devil's Tower, the Black Hills, the Grand Tetons, the Buffalo Bill Museum in Cody Wyoming, and Wall Drug Store . I am glad my parents felt these trips were worthwhile. I had a grand time in the Canadian Rockies when I discovered one of my Berkeley buddies, Rick was there with his family too.

My parents had taken us also to many places on the West coast including La Jolla, Disneyland, the Hearst Castle, Yosemite, Mt. Lassen, the Spanish Monasteries, several UC campuses, Crater Lake, San Francisco, and Portland, OR.

David Thurber Mair adds:

"I recall your father visiting me at San Francisco Seminary in San Anselmo, that summer (I cannot remember if the rest of you were with him on that visit). San Anselmo is north of San Francisco, across the Golden Gate Bridge in Marin County. The seminary is part of a consortium with seminaries in the Berkeley area. Your dad was curious if the degree I was pursuing was a genuine advanced degree program or just some continuing education workshop kind of thing. I convinced him it was a real doctorate, requiring me to show the ability to handle ancient Greek and Hebrew, etc. He then chose to assist me financially with the program for which I have forever been grateful.

My thesis dealt with economic issues, having to do with the views of the Apostle Paul, John Calvin and the Presbyterian Church in America concerning the poor. The thesis was bounced back to me, the readers having cited my weakness in economic theory. I turned to your father, whose doctorate at Princeton was, I believe, in economics. He gave me a few pointers so that my effort made it through on the second try.

My degree is an STD (standing for Latin, something like Scientifica Theologis Doctorus, which, translated, means, Doctor of the Science of Theology). In the Middle Ages Theology was considered the queen of the sciences - it has since been dethroned. Therefore, my degree is an STD. Later on, when I served on the Planned Parenthood board, my colleagues got a kick out of that doctoral title because STD, to them, stood for Sexually Transmitted Diseases.

Chapter VI Easthampton, MA 1967 – 1969

I attended Williston Academy in Easthampton, MA for tenth, eleventh, and twelfth grade. The first two years I was a "day boy." The last year I boarded at the school. That choice was a form of rebellion and an expression of wanting to fit in to the Williston world. These were, as they say, formative years. I was a hippie, an alcohol and drug user, and a protester, but I graduated in the top 10% of my class and was a member of the Cum Laude Society.

I was amazed when I got sober to learn that not everybody drank the way that I and my "friends" did. I think the drugs and alcohol were somehow glamorous then. I was everybody's friend, a preppy hippie! I wasn't a dealer exactly, but I could arrange transactions between my "townie" friends who sold drugs and my "Willie" friends who had the money and the inclination to purchase them. I am not all that sure that this is so different than many business models by which people achieve success in the adult world!

These years involved several trips with Willie friends and Townie friends to NYC and Greenwich Village where the drinking age was 18 and it was happening! I remember Manhattan in a snowstorm. I remember going to the Electric Circus in Greenwich Village.

Let us be honest here. I enjoyed drinking and drugging in my high school days. However, I was young and healthy then and it was easier to recover after a hard night partying. In addition, looking back with hindsight, I can see that my "wasted" youth slowed me down the rest of my life. I thought that my partying connections helped me get into the "in" crowd. I suppose it did, as I perceived it. Today, though, many of that "in" crowd are dead. The squares I looked down on are judges, lawyers, doctors, and corporate executives!

My hippie friends included Dildo Dave, Discount Pete, and Lenny Lettuce. I won't mention their real names as one is now a respected Republican CPA! My preppie friends who I commuted to Williston included John, Tommy, and Mike. John and Mike went back to Northampton High School after one year at Williston. Tommy's mother Frances was active in the Amherst Quaker Meeting and tried to recruit me as a conscientious objector. I found out only recently that Tommy was asked to leave the school before his senior year. At the time, I did not feel I was a conscientious objector, although I later became an active Quaker in 1995.

We hippies hung out in downtown Northampton, MA in a place called Pulaski Park. The dope dealers called it "the office". I found some newspaper articles from the time that I had saved. There was almost a gang war in the Park between the "hippies", the "greasers", and the "jocks". These were meaningful terms, identifying teen sub-cultures at that time. The paper clearly blamed the hippies for the trouble. Hey, we were flower children and we would blame the greasers for invading our turf! We also use to hang out at "Harley's" house (Harley's mom must have been asleep at the wheel) where many hippies crashed. We also spent nights at St. John's Episcopal Church whose doors were always open and where a lot of the hippies slept. At least a couple of times, I visited the house and doctor's office described in “Running with Scissors” since a couple of the kids in that family were hippie friends of mine. And the bizarre things in the movie and book were quite true.

I made a little money working on the Buildings & Grounds crew of Smith College during school vacations and in the summer. This actually became valuable experience when I, semi-retired, become Sexton of the FRS UU Church in Newburyport, MA many years later.

In the summer my family would go to Cape Cod. I lived in a tent in the woods, smoked pot, surfed, and went to P'town (Provincetown) a lot. I saw musicians perform there at a small club called the Blues Bag who I still listen to today: Dave Van Ronk, Richie Havens, Tom Rush, Eric Anderson, and Taj Mahal. I also remember a guy named Jamie Brockett who had a long song about the sinking of the Titanic.

Lila was my first real love and girlfriend. We used to sneak out to the garage to my family’s old 1951 Plymouth. I remember one snowy night when Lila and I hung around the Smith College Campus and then came home and shoveled snow at my house. I walked Lila home and her father (a Palestinian professor at Smith who was a strict father to his oldest daughter) mocked us for “shoveling snow.” It’s funny how I often got accused of things I may have done but at a time when I really didn’t do them.

I guess our parents didn’t want us “going steady”. I remember a couple of incidents that I think were related but I am not sure if they were. I went to a Prom at Our Lady of the Elms a Catholic Girls School in Springfield, MA with Marty whom I mentioned earlier from my time in elementary school. My parents thought it was a good idea and her parents were chaperones at the prom. Marty and I no longer really clicked though. She thought Earnest Hemingway was a “dirty” author and I thought he was great! A few days later Lila went out with my friend Howie and kissed him by Paradise Pond. I heard about it (probably from Howie) and got drunk for the first time on my parents’ liquor. I loved the high although not the aftereffects. I didn't care what Lila did! Ha ha ha.

I remember walking on a cold winter night with Debby holding hands without gloves. The warmth from the two hands was something you could really feel. Note: John mentioned above, and Lila were an item at this time. When John and Lila split up, Lila and I started going out. John tormented me for years after this, going as far as putting my obituary in the local paper. In 1967 my friend Lila (a Palestinian) and my friend Mike (Jewish) had a fist fight in my back yard over the 1967 war. It was probably the first time a realized how bitterly divided some people are.

Today, Lila is an ivy league professor and Mike is a retired news correspondent. Andy Mair, David Thurber Mair's son, was visiting with his family and tagged along on one of my dates with Lila. This didn't work out too well as I recall since my attention was distracted from my cousin! Lila's family moved to Chicago, IL when I was in eleventh grade and that was the end of our short relationship, but we still correspond today. Andy Mair died in a car accident many years later.

I did also have some memorable moments with other girls. During most of my life I have had girls who were friends as well as girlfriends. Maybe this is one of the reasons my significant relationships have usually broken up. However, I would still say there is nothing wrong with friendships with members of the opposite sex even if they are not physical.

Karen was a neighborhood friend. We used to go swimming at the Smith College pool in the summer. One day after swimming as Karen and I were walking home near the Smith College boat house on College Lane we were caught in a sudden downpour. We were soaked but I remember the experience as one of the most joyful moments in my life! And it recalls to mind a much earlier, but vivid memory on College Lane. My mother, sister, and I were visiting the house of the College Chaplain when I was still very young. It was raining and I was staring at the raindrops running down the window. I could not understand how that happened, but I remember a feeling of wonder and awe that I have seldom experienced since.

I recall still yet another experience on College Lane. One day I was smoking marijuana down by Paradise Pond on the Smith College campus that was laced with LSD, which I didn't know until I was already on a semi-bad trip. In retrospect, it was an interesting experience, but I was terrified at the time. I wanted to come down and somehow, I thought citric acid would do the trick, so I decided to go to the Smith College Green House and get a Fresca out of the vending machine. I had to climb up a grassy bank, but it seemed like a vertical brick wall to me. I saw Karen K and Ruth W at the top of the hill near the Green House. I thought I saw them waving scarfs from atop the Wailing Wall in Jerusalem. I climbed the wall and talked to them. I have no idea if I made any sense. I rushed away to get the Fresca (which didn't help by the way). Later I walked home watching lamp posts morphing into witches and similar hallucinations. When I got home, I listened to Jimi Hendrix and went to sleep and when I woke up the effects of the drug had worn off.

Figure 34 Lila and Karen

My senior year I went to Bermuda for spring break. It was a beautiful island. I spent most of my time drinking beer and wooing a young woman named Nancy from Pennsylvania, PA. We rented motor scooters and did tour the island, but what I thought at the time was the greatest thing about Bermuda was that they had "high tea" every day – essentially an early cocktail hour.

I almost was expelled from Williston two weeks before graduation for drinking. I wasn't guilty the night of the incident although I was other nights. I broke my leg about the same time playing in a Senior/Faculty softball game. The teachers thought I was faking so I spent the night in the dorm in excruciating pain. I remember my mother bailed me out of this one and confronted the teachers about their attitude! I was a rebel though and helped lead a march that blocked traffic in front of the headmaster's house. We had a "meeting" with the Headmaster to negotiate terms in his office. He took names. We all got black-balled at Ivy League schools. The issue was "star" athletes getting preferential treatment in assignment of dorm rooms. Peter, one of my best friends, was told to move out of his room so a wrestler could have it.

A week later I graduated on crutches and the platform on which the faculty sat collapsed in the middle of the ceremony. My class was

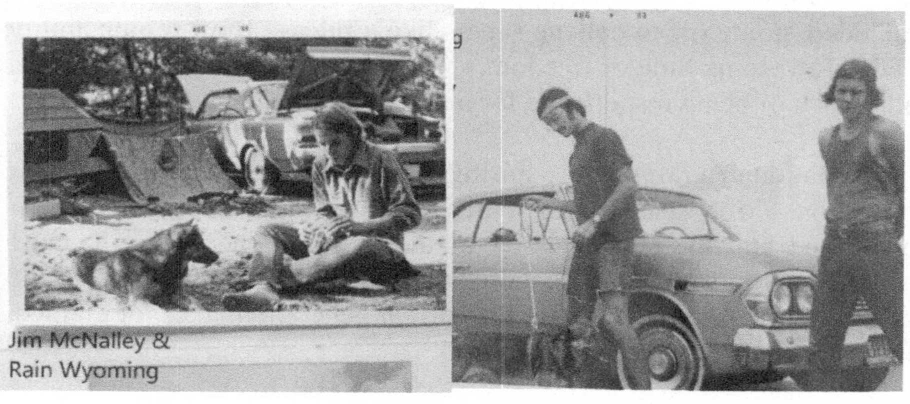

Figure 36 Jim McNally and Rain (dog) in Wyoming in 1969

Figure 35 Peter Clark and Jim McNalley 1969

accused of sawing the legs on the platform but to the best of my knowledge that never happened. Another couple of weeks later, house detectives at a NYC Hotel were pulling me out of a bathtub after I passed out at our graduation party! I ended up barefoot, on crutches, with no money and no wallet on the streets of NYC early in the AM. Somehow, my buddies found me and got me safely home to one of their parent's apartments on the Upper East Side.

That summer I drove to the west coast with my friends Peter and Jim and Jim's dog Rain. We camped out in some great spots including the Grand Tetons. I visited Molly from Berkeley, CA (actually she came to Sausalito where I was staying with another Williston friend, "Wild Thing", Doug S.). We drove back and the guys dropped me off in Beloit, WI where I began my college career at Beloit College.

My senior year in high school marked the transition from being a member of a family to being an independent soul. This is a transition that most people make at some point. I have learned as a parent that this can be a very painful time for a parent and a very confusing time for a child. It is indeed a rite of passage and one that our society may fail in properly acknowledging.

In the Amesbury Friends Meeting we have tried to celebrate this time of life with our Passages program. For some young people, myself included, going off to college seems like a release from responsibility and an awesome time of freedom. Many of us, eventually pick up the adult task of being responsible for our actions.

Participation in a religious or spiritual practice is helpful in making this transition. Most generations remember the "good old days" of their childhood and the superficiality of the newest generation of young adults. I certainly have these thoughts about cell phones, GPS, TV, and many of the other technologies the current generation takes for granted. Progress is not always perfection!

Chapter VIII Beloit WI 1969 – 1973

Figure 37 Sigma Chi, College Row, Beloit, WI

These were my college years at Beloit College in Beloit, WI. The Beloit Plan meant that the school operated year-round including the summer. There were three trimesters each year. The first three trimesters and the last three trimesters you had to spend on campus. You only had to be on campus two of the other six trimesters in the middle. I spent half a year in San Francisco, CA, half a year in Bethesda, MD and after graduation, my ninth trimester in Geneva, Switzerland.

This was an exciting time in my life. The first three months in college were probably the highlight of my life as far as new adventures go. I lived in Hayden Hall with two roommates in two rooms. Jay L. left so Bob J. and I had two rooms for ourselves. It was a close-knit floor and we all got along. Several of the guys had been at Woodstock, NY. I had been in California. We had "beach parties" on the dorm roof, were rushed by several fraternities, and had communal steam baths. We had great concerts at which I worked the old-fashioned klieg lights. Featured acts included: several blues artists, Shan Na Na, and Frank Zappa. There was a Blues Concert featuring Furry Lewis and other older blues artists. I dated three girls and lost my virginity to the sounds of Cream (Disraeli Gears). I was on a natural high for a few days after that.

Those were potent relationships that shaped the rest of my college career and maybe my life, but I won't go into that now.

There was a guy named Farmer John that had a farm near the college. I noted that the senior men were dating freshmen girls so I decided I would date senior women and it worked out well. Bob J. and Tony and Eric and I started to DJ at the college radio station. Tony became Station Manager our senior year, Bob lost interest, but Eric and I got fired for being too outrageous on the air. Bob later became Captain of the Beloit football team which lost every game but one in the four years we were there. But I remember the satisfied look in Bob's eyes the one game they won. I attended a lot of games because I worked as a hotdog vendor at the stadium for a friend.

The drinking age was 21 but in nearby South Beloit, Illinois it was 18 so buying liquor wasn't difficult. I also often borrowed Ken B's driver's license because we looked alike and he was a friend from Williston. He called one day from the police station and asked me if I "could look in his room for his license and bring it down to the station. I did, on his motorcycle! I did a lot of drinking with seniors at the Dahl House and Goodies Bar when I was a freshman. Goodies was old fashioned with sawdust on the floor, hard-boiled eggs on the counter, and a shuffleboard table. All you could order was a liquor and sweet or a liquor and sour, or a draft beer. Once the older guys shamed the bartender into serving me even though I didn't have an ID. I have always felt guilty about that.

I joined two fraternities which is rather unusual. First, I joined Phi Kappa Psi and went through their Hell Week. That Hell Week was based upon the same principal as boot camp. Break the spirit of the individual and build up loyalty to the community (brothers). This fraternity dissolved so the next year I joined Sigma Chi. I must say that their pledge ritual was much better thought out and educational.

I have remained a life member of Sigma Chi.

When I returned to college after two terms in Bethesda, Maryland I decided to become a serious student. I switched majors from English to Government. My Government professors were hard, but I learned a lot from them, especially Milton Feder my advisor. I was elected Student Senate President. One of my campaign tactics was to promise to hold Senate meetings in the Coffee House (an on-campus bar). It must have worked. I was elected and we did have at least one Senate Meeting at the bar. As Student President I was also the student rep to the Board of Trustees and attended Board Meetings in Chicago at the Drake Hotel. That was quite enlightening! I worked hard on my studies these two years and got my average up from C+ to B+ and got a full scholarship to graduate school.

Figure 38 Jane & Susan

Relationships

aI had several girlfriends in college and graduate school, some of whom reentered my life at various times and places in the future. Perhaps this is the time to say that I learned a lot from all these relationships. I regret none of them and value them all as life learning experiences. Jane C, Paola F, and Grace L. will appear again in other chapters.

Figure 39 Jane and Ed in Urbana, IL

I knew Karen and Lila in Northampton, MA when I was at Williston. I knew Jane W. and Susan in college and at graduate school. I met Paola in Barcelona, Spain and she later visited me in Boston, MA and Northampton, MA. Other women friends from college that I remember fondly were Barb, Carlin, Gail, Jan, Linda, Lynn, Mary, Debbie, and Patti.

Figure 40 Ed & Paola

I picked up some bad habits in college like drinking and smoking but I was able to quit both later in life. Although, many factors contributed to my ability to lose these demons, I believe one was the ability to look at the world realistically because of a liberal arts education.

One of my best woman friends was Erica U. Erica typed my papers for me, and we hung out together whenever one of us felt lonely or lost. I have never forgotten Erica.

This didn't save me from a certain narcissism and self-centeredness in relationships. I believe I have improved in this area over time, but I find I am still quite independent rather than codependent. I will never know what it is like to be with one partner for fifty years. On the other hand, I have been privileged to get to know many fine women closely.

My last relationship with Margy is truly one of equals satisfied with each other as companions and responsible for living our own lives. There are some advantages to aging. In my opinion, one of these advantages is being less of a slave to hormones and other internal drugs!

Liberal Arts colleges have a hard time competing with STEM (Science, Technology, Engineering, Mathematics) schools these days. However, I have always valued both my prep school and college educations as opportunities to learn how to learn for the rest of my life.

Chapter IX San Francisco CA 1970 – 1971

Figure 41 Golden Gate, San Francisco, CA

In San Francisco, CA I worked as a Patient Escort at the University of California Medical Center Hospital in my fourth trimester at Beloit College.

I was in San Francisco 1970 – 1971. My girlfriend Grace L came to visit me there. We had a happy visit. Rob and I drove to California and stopped at Grace's house in Scarsdale, NY on Christmas Day. Grace loved the surprise, but her mother was quite annoyed, I think.

In California we rented an apartment on Pierce Street just off Haight Street. The Steve Miller Band lived next door. I worked at the UC Medical Center and had to take a bus to and from work. Rob worked at a photo studio on Haight St. Rob's girlfriend Michelle lived with us. We had several visitors from Beloit College and when we left my friend Smacker moved in. Smacker took over our apartment when we left, and I gather it became a drug dealer's house where the residents used beepers to keep in touch with clients. Smacker died in 1998 and his wife Kathy died several years before that. Drugs.

Gandhi my dog from San Francisco who came back to Beloit College with me. Picture is from College paper of an archaeological dig on the college campus Native American mounds.

Figure 42 Gandhi the Dog 1973

I was terrified of the gunshots in our neighborhood at night. I also had my first real experience with being the "other." We had wanted to rent an apartment conveniently located near the UC Medical Center, but we soon learned all the housing in that neighborhood got rented only to medical students. As a patient escort at the Center I was looked down on by all the professionals. I became friendly with my fellow members of the underclass and made friends with a fellow who worked in the pharmacy. Very handy!

The Journey Not the Destination
I liked climbing up on the roof with a six pack of beer where I felt safer and happier. I had one of my first serious conversations about drinking not solving problems with a visitor named Jeff.

In San Francisco I adopted a dog I named Gandhi. Gandhi lived with me in San Francisco then accompanied me back to Beloit College in Wisconsin. One Christmas Gandhi went back to Northampton, MA with me and then back to Beloit. Gandhi became a popular figure on the campus and was eventually adopted by the Sigma Chi fraternity when I graduated.

While I was in San Francisco I had a dental partial made of gold by a dentist across the Bay in Berkely that my father knew. That partial lasted 40 years unlike my straightened hair that soon gave way to an afro hairsyle.

Figure 43 Marggie and Ed Mair at Smith College Graduation 1974

Chapter X Bethesda, MA 1971-1972

Figure 44 National Institute of Health Bethesda, MD

In Bethesda, MD I was a Normal Volunteer Control Patient at the National Institutes of Health during my sixth and seventh trimesters at Beloit College.

I was in Bethesda 1971-1972. There I broke up with Grace who was in Spain and started dating Jane.

Jane dumped me for a bipolar patient but we later got back together when we both ended up as graduate students in Amherst, MA at University of Massachusetts (UMASS). Several of us took a road trip to Cape Hatteras which is where is where Jane and I first hooked up. After Jane left me, I had a very rewarding platonic relationship with a girl named Katherine from Wilton, CT who was dying of cancer. I held her hand through several tests and she had one of the freest spirits I have ever known. She died soon after I believe.

In 2012 I was interviewed by a professor at Wesleyan College about my experiences at NIH. Well, as I told her we were anything but normal! Plenty of sex, drugs, and rock and roll. We had passes from NIH to prove we weren't junkies since we got stuck with needles a lot. We also were often on 24-hour urine collection so we would take empty gallon milk jugs with us when we went to Georgetown to drink beer. It was a cushy life though most of the time featuring electric beds, remote control TV, and quite good food off a menu when we weren't in a study that restricted nutrition. We also

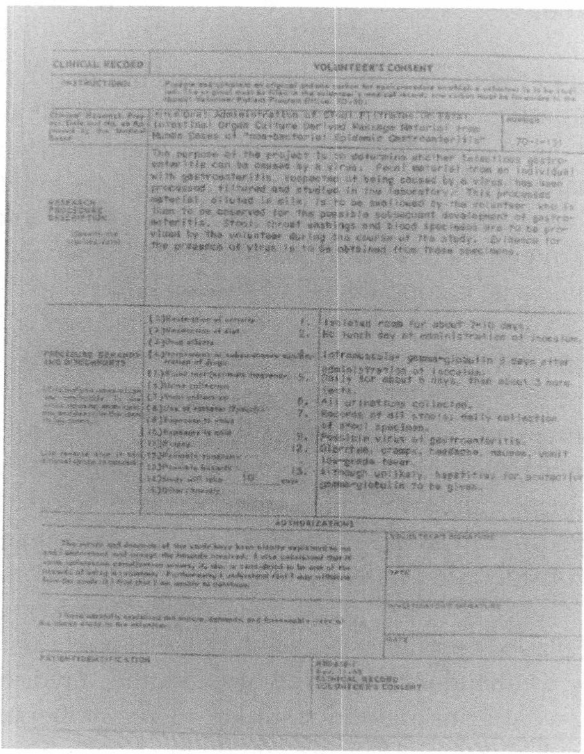

CLINICAL RECORD — VOLUNTEER'S CONSENT

Intestinal Organ Culture Derived Passage Material from Human Cases of "non-bacterial Epidemic Gastroenteritis"

The purpose of the project is to determine whether infectious gastroenteritis can be caused by a virus. Fecal material from an individual with gastroenteritis, suspected of being caused by a virus, has been processed, filtered and studied in the laboratory. This processed material, diluted in milk, is to be swallowed by the volunteer, who is then to be observed for the possible subsequent development of gastroenteritis. Stool, throat washings and blood specimens are to be provided by the volunteer during the course of the study. Evidence for the presence of virus is to be obtained from these specimens.

1. Isolated room for about 7-10 days.
2. No lunch day of administration of inoculum.

Intramuscular gamma-globulin 9 days after administration of inoculum.

5. Daily for about 6 days, then about 3 more tests.
6. All urinations collected.
7. Records of all stools; daily collection of stool specimen.
9. Possible virus of gastroenteritis.
12. Diarrhea, cramps, headache, nausea, vomit, low-grade fever.
13. Although unlikely, hepatitis; for protective gamma-globulin to be given.

AUTHORIZATIONS

Figure 45 NIH Permission Form

got a small stipend and Jane and I rented an apartment in Gaithersburg, MD with another couple.

We had to sign forms for all experiments we participated in. I decided not to participate in the experiment shown below. I did sit in a bathtub full of ice cubes for as long as I could stand it and had my wisdom teeth out while I was there.

One experiment I participated in was having all my wisdom teeth extracted while testing a new method of anesthesia. This method involved an intravenous drip of Valium. I must admit I enjoyed it. The recovery involved injections of painkillers every four hours. I liked that too!

I made one of the more important decisions of my life while I was at NIH in Bethesda. I had spent most of my time at college up until this point partying and having a good time. My grades were only fair. I realized that my parents were spending a lot for my college education and I was not really doing my part. I resolved that when I got back to Beloit College I would work hard and try to succeed as a student. It turned out to be a good decision!

I returned to college in Wisconsin and raised my GPA substantially.

One requirement for government majors was to work on a presidential campaign. I chose to work for Richard Nixon because I heard that the Republicans treated their workers better. That was true as far as getting gifts of food went. Today, of course, my politics take into consideration more than bribes!

Jane and I played contract bridge and I played poker with “the boys.” Swimming in abandoned quarries was another favorite pastime as, of course, were drinking and smoking. I remember Led Zeppelin, Santana, and 10 Years After playing on huge rolls of magnetic tape!

Figure 46 The Matterhorn, Zermatt, Switzerland

Switzerland 1974

Chapter XI Geneva, Switzerland 1973

In Geneva, Switzerland, I studied at the International Labor Organization (ILO), the World Health Organization (WHO), and United Nations Environment Program (UNEP). I had gone there with a group of Beloit College students who were spending our "ninth term" there – after graduation.

Claudio from Peru became my good friend and when he went home, he left me his moped. Claudio and I obtained the key to the wine cellar in our dorm and got drunk on wine almost every night. There were several young women from Smith College who I became friends with. I was in Geneva in the summer of 1973 after which I travelled through Switzerland, Italy, and Spain with two friends, Kent and David, and then met my parents and sister in England. Before I met my parents, I spent a few days in Bishop's Stortford with Sarah whom I had fallen in love with in Geneva. Sarah was with a group of Quaker youth who were studying in Geneva and staying in our dormitory, the Foyer John Knox. We travelled by train to Arolla, the Matterhorn and other scenic Swiss places.

I have many fond memories of Geneva. Eating cheese fondue with a group of friends in the Old City is one of them.

Figure 47 Returning home from Zurich Switzerland

When I returned from Europe I started my two years of graduate school at UMASS – Amherst, as a Massachusetts Senior State Fellow in the M.P.A. program. Everything was paid plus I was given an on-campus office and a stipend. When I look at the debt kids are saddled with these days I am appalled and realize how lucky I was back then in the seventies! Jane was living in Northampton, MA with Susan and we had an on-again off-again relationship.

Figure 48 Library UMASS Amherst, MA

I spent many hours with Jane and her friends Patti and Susan. Later Susan spent a few days with me in Holyoke and I visited her in Olympia, WA. Howie and I attended Tom's wedding in Holyoke.

Chapter XII Amherst, MA 1974

Figure 49 Campus Center UMASS Amherst, MA

Jane was attending UMASS studying Public Health with my Northampton friend Howie B. I was studying Public Administration. I, spent as much time with Jane's roommate Jim, staying up all night and playing RISK. When Jane graduated, she moved to Presque Isle, ME.

I stayed in Boston working at the Department of Public Welfare and then in the HEW Office of Family Planning Services. As an intern, I had the opportunity to visit with the Governor, the Boston State Hospital, the Chelsea Soldiers Home, and to ride in a police car escorting the students to be bussed into South Boston to integrate the schools there. I eventually took a job as Director of Planning and

Development at the New England Farmworkers Council in Springfield, MA and moved to Holyoke, MA.

UMASS was my first exposure to computers and I really liked them. Imagine, we used punch cards and had to turn a "job" in at the computer center and wait 24 hours to see if it worked. If it didn't run, you had to find the mistake and keypunch the cards again and resubmit the cards. I found pre-punched data cards from SPSS which was like finding gold. I remember that I discovered that there was not only a third world but probably a fourth world which included countries like Afghanistan.

Figure 50 Sage Hall, Smith College, Northampton, MA

Amherst, MA

In 1974, because I had a fellowship, I was given an office. My life was bizarre when I look back at it. I pretty much lived and slept in that office. I drank in bars on campus at night and studied very hard during the day.

I graduated with my master's degree with a 4.0 average and as a confirmed alcoholic I believe.

Figure 51 Ed and George Fisk Mair shoveling snow at 57 Washington Ave. Northampton, MA

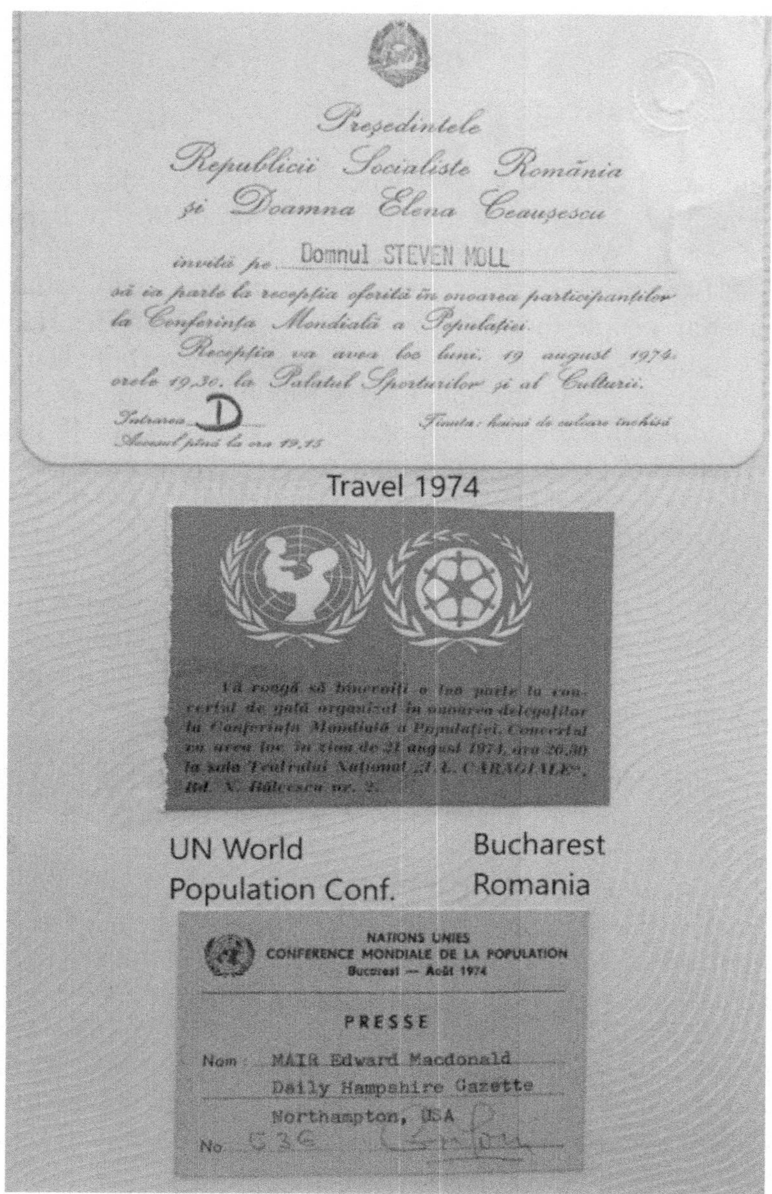

Președintele
Republicii Socialiste România
și Doamna Elena Ceaușescu

invită pe Domnul STEVEN MOLL
să ia parte la recepția oferită în onoarea participanților la Conferința Mondială a Populației.
Recepția va avea loc luni, 19 august 1974, orele 19,30, la Palatul Sporturilor și al Culturii.

Intrarea D
Accesul până la ora 19,15
Ținuta: haină de culoare închisă

Vă rugăm să binevoiți a lua parte la concertul de gală organizat în onoarea delegaților la Conferința Mondială a Populației. Concertul va avea loc în ziua de 21 august 1974, ora 20,30 la sala Teatrului Național „I. L. CARAGIALE", Bd. N. Bălcescu nr. 2.

NATIONS UNIES
CONFERENCE MONDIALE DE LA POPULATION
Bucarest — Août 1974

PRESSE

Nom: MAIR Edward Macdonald
Daily Hampshire Gazette
Northampton, USA
No. 536

Figure 52 Documents from 1974 Trip to Romania

Amherst, MA

Chapter XIII Bucharest Romania 1974

I went back to Europe in 1974 when I received a fellowship to be a student representative at the United Nations World Population Conference, . We studied in Lucerne, Switzerland and then took the Orient Express to Bucharest, Romania. I ate meals with some really interesting people there: Casper Weinberger, Alexander Haig, and Margaret Mead. I wrote Newspaper stories for the Daily Hampshire Gazette back in Northampton. This was while Romania was still communist and under Nicholas Ceausescu. We had a VIP pass that let us into all the elite clubs, and we attended a reception at the President's Palace. I have some very good memories of this trip, but I was drinking a lot too!

We split our large group into smaller groups. I purposely chose to be in a group that was more there for an adventure than to study. In the group were Michael, Marcos, Maybelline, Maritza, and Larry. We bought marijuana in Budapest, Hungary, slept over at a family's home in Bern, Switzerland, and had a great ride on the Orient Express to Bucharest from Luzern. One of my fondest memories is Maritza brushing my hair for what seemed like hours as the train rolled along.

In Bucharest, I was almost seduced by a maid in the hotel and I was scammed by a Dutch fellow my own age who I lent a bed to and who disappeared with most of my money. I should have been smarter. His belief system was "anything goes!" We took a side trip to the Caspian Sea which is as far east as I have ever been! Steve Moll was my roommate who gave me his invitation to the President's palace when I lost mine. I stole two bottles of vodka within sight of guards with machine guns.

I was appalled at the way Gypsies were treated in Romania.

Chapter XIV Boston, MA 1975

Figure 53 JFK Federal Building, Boston, MA

The second year of the MPA program was spent in Boston, MA I lived briefly near Cleveland Circle with Ruth then near the

Boston, MA 1975

Museum of Fine Arts with Tom B. and Howie. Finally, after being robbed three times Howie and I moved to Pleasant Street in Arlington and Tom moved back to Northampton.

Several friends I had met in Europe visited: Sarah and Moustafa, Paola and Giovanna, Susan and Tom. Howie and I hung out with Ruth and Laurie. Howie remembers walking by a pet store on fire and I tried to crawl in and save the pets. I didn't remember this; I was probably drunk. He thought it was heroic, when he mentioned it to me several years later. I did remember the thick black suffocating smoke and I am thankful I got back out alive!

Howie and I went to Thanksgiving in Newton with Paola's cousin who was checking us out. Paola and Giovanna were from Italy and were staying with us.

It turned out Paola's sister was married to an official at the Italian Embassy in Washington, DC. I was invited to a New Year's Eve party at the Italian Embassy. I never made it! My train from Boston, MA got diverted by an accident. We had quite a party on the train in the bar car, but we didn't get in until after midnight. I was quite inebriated, and I stumbled into the first fleabag hotel I could find. The guy at the desk asked me if I wanted him to send up a girl and a bottle. I said no and went upstairs and passed out. I did connect first with my friend from Williston Peter, and then with Paola. I am not sure what Paola thought of my story, but we remained friends for several more years. She and her husband later came and visited with my wife and myself in Newburyport, MA

Pets

It was while living in Arlington that I adopted my first pet cats. I found Sarah and Erica as kittens at a rest area in Gardener, MA. They were hungry and scared and I just found myself unable to leave them there. Gandhi (a handsome mix) and Maisy (a cockapoo) were solo residents for a while. But many of my pets seem to come in pairs. For many years my cats were Sneakers and Nickels. More recently we have had Chloe (a black golden doodle)) and Chelsea (a cat), followed by Argo and Venus. (cats).

Chapter XV Russia, Ukraine, Armenia, Georgia, Azerbaijan 1976

In 1976 I went on an exchange visit to the USSR with the American Society of Public Administration. We visited with city officials in Moscow, Kiev (Ukraine), Tbilisi (Georgia), Yerevan (Armenia), and Baku (Azerbaijan). All these republics were at that time part of the U.S.S.R. It is the only time I have been in the Middle East or Asia. I am glad I got to see communism firsthand because I certainly didn't like what I saw.

My roommate John got involved with our Russian guide and we visited with some locals and no doubt were carefully watched as well. Every floor in the hotels we stayed in had "firemen" on duty.

The summer before I had been working at the Hotel Northampton, living at home, and dating Smith college girls. Several of my friends from Williston and Northampton were living in the area. It is ironic that the skills I picked up then such as mopping, and painting have turned out to be the skills I used as a Sexton at the First Religious Society UU in my sixties. Life is a circle!

Figure 54 University of Moscow, USSR 1975

I was particularly impressed by the monumental architecture in these countries. I learned about many historical events such as the genocide in Armenia in the early 20th century.

Figure 56 Baku, Azerbaijan City Hall

Figure 55 Baku Azerbaijan view from Maiden's Tower

Russia, Ukraine

The food was bad. I came to have a dislike for cucumbers and cilantro that seemed to be served with every meal, even breakfast. Many types of vodka flowed freely, and we shopped at U.S. dollar stores. Something like beer was sold from vending machines on the streets.

Figure 57 Red Pioneers in Ukraine SSR 1975

Chapter XVI Holyoke, MA and Boise, ID 1976–1978

Home Boise, Idaho 1978-19

Figure 59 House in Boise Idaho

Figure 58 Boise, Idaho

Boise, ID

In 1976 I lived in Holyoke, MA in two apartments. First, I lived in a garden apartment with two cats along the Connecticut River in Smith's Ferry. I was kicked out of here because of the cats and moved to a downtown tenement apartment on the fourth floor. My cousin Peter from Scotland and others visited me here. I worked at the New England Farm Workers' Council in Springfield, MA where I met Betsy.

1977 was the year that Betsy and I moved to Idaho. I was invited to join the Idaho Migrant Council having previously met the leaders of that organization as a member of the Board of the National Association of Farmworker Organizations. Betsy attended Nursing School at Boise State College. I loved Idaho. The Birds of Prey Area in the Snake River Canyon was right down a dirt road from our house in the desert in Kuna. Also, on our dirt road were the Idaho State Penitentiary and the National Guard training grounds. Some mornings we would awake to clouds of dust as National Guard tanks rolled past our house

We soon bought a house in Boise proper, but the quality of life was good there as well. Betsy attended nursing school at Boise State College, and I helped with Senator Ted Kennedy's 1980 presidential campaign.

I oversaw projects in Idaho, Oregon, Washington, Montana, and Colorado. I frequently flew between our offices in Caldwell, Nampa, Twin Falls, and Burley and went to the Rio Grande in Texas about twice a year and to Washington, DC about 4 times a year. Betsy was stuck in the desert in Idaho most of the time when I travelled, and I don't think she loved living in the desert in Idaho as much as I did. So, we bought a small but cute bungalow home in Boise for $39,000. We sold it two years later for $59,000. (Our first home in Newburyport in 1980 cost $75,000. Hard to believe these days! 1978 was a big year of transitions. Betsy and I returned to New Jersey and were married in June. We got married in Allendale N.J. at the home of her parents Stiles and Lillian. We had two separate events. The actual wedding to which we invited mostly non-drinking older relatives and a large reception under a tent where there were a lot of guests and a lot of drinking!

My father was ill with cancer at that time. But I could tell he was happy about our wedding. After our honeymoon in Florida and the Keys, I spent a weekend in the mountains above Bakersfield, CA with the NAFO Board and Caesar Chavez and the United Farmworkers Board.

I truly enjoyed Idaho. Back then in Boise, ID the capitol city, many people already heated with thermal hot water. There were mountains and desert, hot springs, and 300 days of sunshine a year. You could drift from one end of town to the other in an inner tube on the Boise River passing through several downtown parks on the way. The offices of the Idaho Migrant Council where I worked were in the same building with the public library and I could ride my bike to work. Boise had several good restaurants and our Board of Directors

Figure 60 Ed at Betsy and Ed's Wedding

meetings were conducted in Spanish and held in places like Ketchum, ID and Sun Valley. I spent many happy hours with co-workers at happy hours.

One of my favorite statistics at this time was that while Massachusetts had 600 people per square mile, Idaho had only 6 people per square mile. I am not a city boy!

Another popular saying in the late seventies was "Idaho is what Colorado was."

When I drove on back roads, I always had a case of beer with me. There was little traffic and I never got a ticket for driving under the influence. I visited many bird watching spots on these trips including Silver City, a ghost town. I also visited the Bruneau Sand dunes, Lake Lowell, Craters of the Moon park, and various locations along the Snake River.

I also travelled farther afield to Yakima, WA, Salt Lake City, UT, Greely, CO, Las Vegas, NV, Portland, OR, Seattle, WA, and Bakersfield, CA.

One of my most vivid memories is of walking into the men's room of the State Capitol building and standing at a urinal next to the Governor. Idaho was a very egalitarian state back then, or so it seemed to me.

I returned to Massachusetts in July 1978 and spent a week with my parents at Cape Cod. On September 12, my father died. I had returned about a week before and spent most of the last week of his life with him

George Fisk Mair (1922-1978)

Figure 61 George Fisk Mair

I will devote the rest of this section to my father's life which I think was remarkable! One thing I learned through his death was that immortality entails, at least in part, the ideas and values that we have passed on while we live. We depart, but often our wisdom carries on in our descendants. So too do incorrect behaviors we learn from our parents. Whatever strong values I have or original ideas I have, are in part the values and ideas of my father.

George Fisk Mair was born in 1922 in the Bronx, NY. He attended Riverdale Day School and Princeton University where he earned both a Bachelor's and a PhD. Degree. He was a first lieutenant in WWII and his first job that I know of was as a lecturer at Princeton University. He married my mother, Jean Lois Baum on December 27, 1947 at the First Presbyterian Church in Princeton during a snowstorm. He died September 12, 1978 of cancer in Northampton, MA. At that time, he was Dean of Smith College. Along the way he was a visiting professor at Harvard University, UC Berkeley, the Assistant to President Thomas Mendenhall at Smith and the Smith College representative on the 5-college coordinating committee (Smith College, Mt. Holyoke College, the University of Massachusetts-Amherst, Amherst College and Hampshire College).

He was very bright. I remember him helping me with Math and Latin homework and he still remembered stuff from his childhood that I couldn't remember from the day before! He was brought up in the manse attached to the Bedford Park Presbyterian Church in the Bronx where his father, the Reverend George Mair was minister. He spent much of his adult life as a Deacon and Choir member of the First Congregational Church in Northampton, and he died a Unitarian.

His memorial service was attended by 500 people and officiated at by three ministers: Richard Unsworth the Smith Chaplain, Tex Mosher the Congregational Minister, and John Farmakis the Unitarian minister. Eulogies were given by two Smith College Presidents he worked closely with.

Tom Mendenhall said, "George Mair had the rare but essential ability to rise above personal or departmental concerns and achieve a larger college perspective on every question…For me the common denominator in this good man, whom the Smith community will miss so much, was his moderation."

Jill Kerr Conway said, “In 1974 when I first began to visit Smith College…to a wide variety of questions about how things worked people would invariably answer, ‘You’d best ask George Mair that’…. The team that worked beside him in College Hall felt their lives illuminated by the clarity of his intellect, by the honesty of his emotions, and the strength of his commitment to tasks and to people.”

If, since his death I have been able to keep any of his ideas alive or been able to put into practice any of the lessons he taught me, then I can say I have succeeded in life! As his faculty colleagues wrote in a memorial in the Smith Alumnae Newsletter after his death. “George Mair was not a college character; he was character itself.”

The Statement of Purpose of the Free Congregation Society of Florence, MA written in 1863 and often attributed to Sojourner Truth was also read at his memorial service.

> “Respecting in each other and in all the right of intellect and conscience to be free, and holding it to be the duty of everyone to keep his mind and heart at all times open to receive the truth and follow its guidance, we set up no theological condition of membership and neither demand nor expect uniformity of doctrinal belief, asking only unity of purpose to seek and accept the right and true and an honest aim and effort to make these the rule of life; and recognizing the brotherhood of the human race and the equality of human rights, we make no distinction as to the conditions and rights of membership in this society on account of sex, or color, or nationality.”

In 1980 Betsy and I drove back across the country with our two cats, Sarah and Erica, taking the furthest northern route we could through Montana and North Dakota. We had intended to drive from northern Michigan through Canada, but we couldn’t cross the border with the

Boise, ID

Figure 63 Duncaster, Bloomfield, CT

I came back East to work for the federal government at the JFK Building in Boston. Later I worked for the State of Massachusetts at the Saltonstall Building peeking out behind the JFK Building.

Figure 62 Boston, MA

Sarah and Erica, our cats, so we drove through Michigan, Illinois, Indiana, and Pennsylvania until we reached Allendale, NJ where Betsy's parents lived. I remember that after three years in Idaho, the traffic and congestion of the East was a real shock to me.

Chapter XVII Newburyport, MA 1980-1982

I had promised Betsy that if she didn't like it in Idaho after two years, I would look for a job back east. She didn't like Idaho so I tried to find a job back east. I later found out that I was selected as #24 out of 26 successful applicants out of 400 total applicants for a year as a US Department of Health and Human Services Fellow. Thus, I got a job that took me to Washington, DC and Boston, MA as a Special Assistant to Secretary of Health and Human Service (DHHS), first, Patricia Roberts Harris (D) and later Richard Schweiker (R). I even had tea at the White House with Roslyn Carter! I was a GS-13. I didn't realize it at the time but that was probably the peak of my career in a conventional sense. Disaster struck in the form of the election of Ronald Reagan. Instead of securing a good job with the Department as I expected, I learned the valuable lesson that all things are transient, especially in politics! I was let go by the Reagan administration.

When we came back East, Betsy had stayed with her parents. I stayed in Arlington, MA with Bill (my best man at my wedding) and his wife Patricia. Patricia and I went house hunting in the North Shore area and Betsy and I bought a house in Newburyport while Bill and Patricia bought a house in Merrimacport. We drifted apart for many years, but we still see each other at several year intervals. Bill, Patricia, and I are all cancer survivors and Bill has lived with the disease for several years now.

While I was living in Arlington I commuted by bus and the T (subway) to Boston. I heard the news one morning in the T subway station in Harvard Square that John Lennon had been shot. This really upset me as it seemed to be the end of the age of innocence.

Betsy and I attended a memorial service at Trinity Church in Boston that weekend.

Newburyport, MA

On my last day at DHHS in Boston, MA I was depressed. I left early and went to Durgin Park and had a few martinis. Then I rode the commuter bus home and had a few more. I later found out that the HHS had a going away party for me that I had missed!

I was unemployed for a few months which I really found depressing. I eventually got a job with the Social & Economic Opportunity Office in State Government through a fellow graduate of the UMASS MPA program. Jim, who had stayed on after his internship, had become Director of Administration for the Executive Office of Communities and Development (EOCD). Jim was at my wedding and died a couple of years back.

While unemployed I had started attending a program sponsored by the Department of Unemployment Assistance to teach unemployed workers new computer skills. This really paid off for me and lead to a career in using computers in community service organizations. I bought an Apple II computer (no hard drive, two 51/4" disk drives) and taught myself how to use it. I later wrote a book published by Prentice Hall (1984) called <u>A Field Guide to Personal Computers for Birdwatchers</u>. I also founded the Newburyport Birders Exchange (NBE) which had members in 35 states and five countries. I published a newsletter for Bird Watchers who used computers for five years. I had several articles published in Bird Watchers Digest and Computer magazines.

The Secretary of EOCD at that time was Byron Matthews, a former Mayor of Newburyport when the city went through its award-winning redevelopment. I interviewed with Byron for a job as State Coordinator of Joe Kennedy's bulk oil program. During the interview I told Byron that I wanted to continue my computer training in Lawrence, MA in the program I mentioned above. He said he had no problem with a young man who wanted to better himself, so we shook hands and I got the job. I will always be grateful for his understanding at that time.

My perspective and Joe Kennedy's (his staff) perspective on how the program should be run differed. This was probably my greatest lesson in how politics work. Byron arranged a meeting with Governor Ed King, Joe Kennedy, himself, and I at the Governor's office. When we sat down the Governor said something like, "Good of you to come Ed and Byron. Joe and I just had breakfast and a good talk, and this is how it's going to be." That was the end of the conversation right there! I have remained a fan of the Kennedy's because I think they do work for the best interests of people less fortunate than themselves. However, I learned then, that even the "good guys" in politics play hardball to get what they want!

I went from Coordinator of the bulk oil program to Special Projects Director and set up three computer training programs across the State for the staff of Community Action Agencies. They were in Plymouth, Lowell, and at Holyoke Community College. I travelled among these training sites hiring teachers and arranging facilities for the classes and doing the enrollment paperwork for the admitted students. I taught a few classes myself. At this time Betsy was attending Northern Essex Community College to become an RN. Then she worked in Lowell and Haverhill as a nurse.

This was probably my most active time as a bird watcher, especially as an observer of hawk migration. I was on the Board of the Eastern Massachusetts Hawk Watch, Coordinator of the Plum Island (spring) and West Newbury Page School (fall) hawk watch and NE Regional Editor for the Hawk Migration Association of North America. Betsy and I had gone bird watching in the Everglades and the Florida Keys for our Honeymoon and we made a trip with her parents to Arizona to watch birds. I visited the Rio Grande Valley in Texas several times to watch hawks, give talks, and at first in conjunction with my work with farm workers.

Newburyport, MA

Plum Island was and is a mecca for US bird watchers. I started watching birds here long before I moved there. It is only about two miles from the center of Newburyport. It may be best known for Snowy Owls that come here most winters.

Figure 64 Christmas Card. Picture taken in Lubbock, Texas

Kathryn Conover September 20, 1893 (Pt. Pleasant, NJ) - September 15, 1981 (Northampton, MA

This is about my mother's mother. "Nana" was always the most affectionate relative in the family. She would bestow big hugs and kisses during visits with her grandchildren. I regret now to say that this behavior was frowned upon and merely tolerated in my family. Today, looking back, I am very grateful for this strain of DNA!

Figure 65 Nana Baum with her parents and daughter

Newburyport, MA

Kathryn Baum was mostly of Dutch extraction. I have come to believe that her grandmother Rachel Borden (1848-1937) was a Quaker because of my mother's description of her as a peculiar woman who always wore a bonnet and her ancestry of Bordens and Claytons extending back to Swarthmore Hall in England.

Nana's parents were Frederick Conover (1866-1948) and Elsie Van Note (1871-1963). Conover was a short English change of the original Dutch name of Van Kouwenhoven. Thus, my daughter has a lot of Dutch blood through both of her grandmothers. Frederick was a well to do hardware and lumber merchant in Pt. Pleasant, NJ from what I can find. Pt Pleasant is a town on the Jersey shore hit hard by Hurricane Sandy in 2012.

Kathryn married Granville Baum (1891-1928) from the Norfolk, VA area. He died in 1928 leaving Kathryn to raise my mother, then nine, by herself. The small family moved several times following Kathryn's career as a school teacher, but my research suggests that they lived many winters in Princeton, NJ and several summers in the Virginia Beach area of Virginia. The Baums were a prominent early family in both tidal Virginia and on the outer banks of NC where they owned thousands of acres of land, much of it devoted to market hunting for waterfowl.

One of my earliest memories was watching TV and the 1956 Melbourne Olympics in my Grandmother Baum's second floor apartment near the corner of Nassau and Harrison Streets in Princeton, NJ. I also recall my grandmother taking me on excursions to Pt. Pleasant beach and buying me ice cream sandwiches. Such things as TV and ice cream were not available in my somewhat Puritan home!

My grandmother also gave my sister and me each $1,000, the only substantial gift of money I remember from my childhood. I remember eagerly looking forward to receiving the annual 5% interest on that gift each year!

In the late 1970s my grandmother was living in Jamesburg, NJ at a place called Leisure World. My wife Betsy was from Allendale, NJ and my other grandmother Evelyn Thurber Mair lived in Hightstown NJ at Meadow Lakes, an assisted living community. So, I made many trips to NJ. It became evident that Kathryn could no longer really live alone. My mother couldn't deal with major events, so I became primary caretaker of my grandmother with assistance from my sister Marggie. We moved "Nana" from NJ to the Lathrop Nursing Home in Northampton, MA. I sold her car and condo in New Jersey and gave the condo money to my mother. She insisted that the car money also belonged to her, but I kept it as reimbursement for my expenses in making several trips to NJ to take care of my grandmother's affairs.

Both my father and my grandmother left substantial estates entirely to my mother. For a while I resented this since my sister, and I did all the work and got nothing. However, in later years, my AA sponsor Rich pointed out, correctly, that at least we didn't have to support my mother and we knew she would be able to take care of herself for life. My mother travelled the world and she lived at a first-class retirement community, but my sponsor was right. It was a real blessing not to have to worry about her financially.

Ironically, I was at Cape May, NJ hawk watching the September day when my grandmother died in Massachusetts. I cut my trip short and returned home. My grandmother's service was held at the First Church in Northampton in which I grew up and which she had joined when she moved to Northampton. Her wish was to be cremated but my mother insisted on buying a coffin and having a viewing at a funeral home. She took photos of the open casket and then allowed a cremation to take place. Fortunately, I was able to be tolerant of this although the whole process made me quite angry!

I took my grandmother's ashes and my mother to New Jersey. My mother's cousin and his wife, Joan Vallance (1927-2006) and John

Newburyport, MA

Allen Potts (1926-1987), joined us for a memorial service at White Lawn Cemetery in Pt. Pleasant. I read a poem my grandmother had written and cried, surprising myself. Today I and my cousin Joanne Potts Michealree (Allen and Joan's daughter) are both genealogy enthusiasts.

My mother and grandmother had a rocky relationship. After, my grandmother died, as after my father died, my mother expressed regret at how she had treated her mother sometimes. I suppose this is not unusual at such times, but I know I learned from my grandmother's ability to be warm and affectionate and from my mother's regrets.

Figure 66 Jean Baum Mair in Wedding Dress 1947

Chapter XVIII Working for the State of Massachusetts and for Community Teamwork, Inc. in Lowell, Ma 1982 – 1990

1982-1984

I finished computer school and worked for the State full time in the Department of Housing and Communities and Development (DHCD). From 10 Milk Street we moved into the Saltonstall Building at 100 Cambridge Street in Boston. I remember looking at my fellow state workers in the elevator and thinking how depressed they all looked and determined I wouldn't spend the next thirty years of my life working there! They, of course, have nice big pensions now but at the cost of thirty years of life I would say. When you are a state worker nobody respects you including the people you serve and the taxpayers who pay for it. It is in some ways very unfair to many hard-working people, but there are plenty of political hacks as well.

I did a lot of bird watching at Plum Island, Salisbury State Park, the NH Seacoast, the Maine seacoast and in other locations. I discovered and established two hawk watching spots: The Parker River Wildlife Refuge Parking Lot #1 in the spring and Page School in West Newbury, MA in the fall. We had American Kestrels, Peregrine Falcons, and Sharp-shinned Hawks at Plum Island and Broad-winged Hawks and Osprey at Page School. The record at the Page School was over 4,000 Broad-winged hawks in one afternoon.

I commuted five days a week on Kinson Bus lines to Boston. I often rode with Leigh S., a childhood friend of Betsy's. Betsy and I became pretty good friends with Leigh and her husband Doug for a few years.

1984 – 1986

1984. Let's see, that George Orwellian year is far in the past now. That year I began to work in Lowell, MA at Community Teamwork Inc., where I was Assistant Director of the Energy Program and eventually IT Director. Betsy and I planned that we would each work three days a week and be off four days a week so we could have a child, and both be home, or at least one of us would be home every day.

Figure 67 Diner next to 167 Dutton Street Lowell, MA

In 1985, I got serious about giving up alcohol prior to having a child. I went to see a counselor with Betsy who suggested that I either go to one AA meeting or go away for a month to a treatment program. At the time going away for a month seemed easier and perhaps it was. Anyway, my one month stay at Spofford Hall in New Hampshire worked and I went to a 12 Step meeting the first day I got back. It wasn't as simple as I make it sound here! I was a high bottom drunk, I hadn't lost everything, and I had to convince my boss I had a problem and needed to treat it. I did convince him I guess, and CTI was very supportive during the month while I was gone and held my job for me when I came back. I think that paid off business wise because I certainly returned as a hardworking, very grateful employee!

Alex George Mair was born four months after I got sober in January of 1986. I still think her birth is probably the most memorable event of my life! A friend 's wife was giving birth the same time as Betsy and as I recall he and I slipped away from the hospital for a meeting but were both back for the births of our respective daughters. Alex hated her middle name, but I have always been glad we named her after my father. It has become the only legacy Mair name in our family.

Alex was what they call or did call a colicky baby. She cried all day every day. A silver lining is that she slept through the night usually. During my days at home I would strap her in a snuggly to my chest and take long walks on the beach or at Maudsley Park. I played a lot of Cyndi Lauper tapes in the car and Alex seems to like Cyndi Lauper songs today.

We would put her to sleep in a basket on the washing machine or play white noise on a tape which seemed to relax her. Anyway, she

Figure 68 Alex and Ed in Epping, NH

outgrew the crying although I would say she remains extremely sensitive to sound and smells!

We lived in a turn of the century Victorian (1900) farmhouse near Atkinson Common in Newburyport where I enjoyed walking with Alex and later going there with her when she was riding a tricycle. We had two cats, Sarah and Erica, and Alex is still fond of cats. She has had several of her own since then.

I went to a lot of 12 Step meetings and smoked a lot of cigarettes in those days. I wrote a book A Field Guide to Personal Computers for Bird Watchers published in 1985. I was quite into bird watching and wrote an article called "Birding with Baby" that was published in the Bird Watcher's Digest. My publisher. Prentice–Hall, suggested I turn this into another book, but I backed out when they told me they wanted to change the title to "Bird watching with children from infancy to High School. I don't think I could write that book now let alone when Alex was a baby!

Figure 69 Alex on Plum Island

We went to New Jersey for Christmas with Betsy's family every year. Betsy was working as a nurse by 1986. I loved to drive the back roads between Lowell and Newburyport. I still prefer back roads, even on long trips. They are much more scenic and interesting than Interstate highways.

Figure 70 Evelyn Thurber Mair in her Wedding Gown 1921

Evelyn Thurber Mair June 25, 1898 (New York City) - April 9, 1989 (Hightstown, NJ)

It was at my grandmother's funeral that I first became aware of my roots in Newbury, MA. My great uncle Gerrish Thurber (1907 - 2000) asked me where I lived, when I told him Newburyport, he said, "Why your ancestor William Gerrish (1617-1687) lived there! You should look him up sometime!" I did five years later and genealogy has become a passion of mine since discovering that, in fact, I have 16 ancestors among the First Settlers of Newbury where I now live. Another surprise at that time was how beautiful middle New Jersey is in the spring. April 9 was the day of my grandmother's death and the day of my mother's birth and the two didn't really like each other.

I had driven to New Jersey with my three-year-old daughter Alex. I imagine she does not remember the trip. We stopped in Valhalla, NY at Kensico Cemetery where we laid some flowers from a bouquet on my father's grave. We later placed the remainder of the bouquet on my grandmother's grave in Ewing, NJ. I also remember that we watched ET on the TV in our motel room.

Evelyn was born in comfortable New York Society. Her father was a doctor in NYC and her mother was the daughter and sister of Harvey Fisk & Sons, Wall Street bankers. The Harvey Fisk (1831-1890) family lived in an estate on the banks of the Delaware River. The train station, Wilburtha was named after two of his children including my great grandmother Bertha Fisk (1874-1958). The Fisk summer home is now a Catholic Girls School called Villa Victoria.

Evelyn's father Dr. Samuel Wood Thurber (1867-1926) died young. Her mother spent her last years in Princeton, NJ in an apartment in Palmer Square. Evelyn married the Rev. George Mair (1885-1962) an immigrant from Aberdeen, Scotland who worked his way through the Mt. Hermon School, Wesleyan College, and Harvard University. He later attended Union Theological Seminary in New York City and became pastor of the Bedford Park Presbyterian Church for nearly 40 years. Evelyn had three children, only one of whom, my Uncle David Thurber Mair (1928-2015), survived her.

During the last days of my father's life, as he lay at the Smith College Infirmary dying of cancer, my grandmother Evelyn and I shared a moment of deep grief in the car after visiting my father. We both cried and, in this moment, I felt for perhaps the only time a connection with this somewhat reserved aristocratic grandmother. It is a moment I will always remember.

The two pieces of furniture that I truly value are my grandfather Mair's desk from Bedford Park and my grandmother Thurber's Secretary. The Secretary dates to 1838 when it was a wedding gift to my great great grandmother Lydia Gerrish (1818-1866) in Boscawen, NH who married Samuel Wood (1807-1889). Samuel later married Samuel Wood's daughter's husband 's mother Mary Bartlett Gerrish Thurber (1815-1884). In addition, Samuel Wood's mother was Sarah Gerrish (1766-1839). This is where the Gerrish family really get into our ancestry!

Towards the end of her life Evelyn Thurber lived at Meadow Lakes in Hightstown, NJ and was very active in the First Presbyterian Church in Princeton, NJ. I remember her often arranging flowers at the Church which is something I enjoyed doing as part of my job as Sexton at the Unitarian Church of Newburyport, MA.

1986-1990

Several important things happened during these years! I spent a good deal of time with my daughter, I worked hard in Lowell, and I stayed sober.

Plum Island

In 1988 Betsy and I campaigned for Michael Dukakis, but ironically Alex often chanted, “George Bush, he’s my man!”

Betsy and I separated. I moved out in October 1989 to a small cottage on Plum Island. Alex spent the weekends there with me. I think she still remembers that you could sneak from one bedroom to another through the two rooms adjoining closets. The house was heated with one giant heater under a grate in the living room and was a short walk from the beach near the Parker River Refuge.

Figure 71 Carly, Ed, and Alex, Amesbury, MA

Figure 72 Bob and Maisy by Peg McIntosh

I had several friends that watched out for me during this lonely time. That is one way the 12 step programs works. Unfortunately, some of these people are no longer sober, and a couple died from the disease of alcoholism. But I had support when I needed it and I am quite grateful for that!

Figure 73 Ed & Vinette

Figure 74 Friends in Amesbury in Parachute

Anonymity in press, radio, and TV is one of the main traditions of many 12 step programs. These are programs like Alcoholics Anonymous, Al-anon, Adult Children of Alcoholics, Debtors Anonymous, Emotions Anonymous, Gamblers Anonymous, Narcotics Anonymous, Nicotine Anonymous, and Overeaters Anonymous. I wish to honor these traditions so I shall not identify myself or anybody else with any specific programs. However, I will say that my life has been infinitely better, and more serene because of the 12 step programs and the friends I have made there. If you think you might have an addiction problem, I highly recommend these 12 Step programs as not only helpful but also eventually enjoyable. 24-hour meetings are conducted on Thanksgiving, Christmas, and New Year's Eve in many locations for people who may have trouble with these holidays.

Figure 75 Home on Plum Island before Addition

When Betsy and I separated I moved to Plum Island. The house I soon purchased was small but had a distant ocean view in the front and a small wood in the back. It was a perfect place for a birdwatcher and over the years I turned the property into a small bird sanctuary. The house has been enlarged, and the ocean view slowly disappeared as the houses between me and the ocean became McMansions blocking the view. Nonetheless, Margy and I still enjoy living here all year (2019) We have a garden, feed the birds, and enjoy the sunrises and sunsets. In retirement the snow is not a big issue!

Chapter XIX Plum Island, MA 1990 – 2000

These were the years immediately following my first divorce. When I look back, they were filled with women and travel. Some of the relationships were platonic and others were not. Generally, I find that most people that have been part of my life taught me something or helped me make important decisions like quitting smoking or drinking or becoming unabashedly religious or placing my daughter ahead of all women in my life!

I first rented an apartment for the winter on Plum Island. Later with the help of my mother I bought a small house at 24R Columbia Way.

I dated Daisy in a rebound relationship. This did not end well.

I lived with Mary Ann and her golden retriever Dugan as my roommates on Plum Island. I spent some time with Vinette, an artist, and Kathy a fellow worker at CTI. Vinette and I had long talks lasting all night.

All these women were interesting people and, in my eyes, very beautiful. I learned a lot from all of them. It seems to me that serial monogamy is a realistic alternative to a single marriage although it seems to be difficult to navigate and remain friends with all one's past partners. I first got this idea from one of my wives. Fortunately, I have remained friends with most of these women as well as others I mention elsewhere.

Every other weekend and Tuesday nights I spent with Alex and often with her best friend Carly and some of her other friends who seemed to enjoy sleep overs with Alex at Plum Island. I explored Plum Island and took long solitary walks on the beach. And commuted by bus, train, and car to Lowell and then Lynn.

Florida

I made three trips to Florida during these years. Once with Marcia to Cedar Key. Once with Daisy to St. Petersburg and once by myself to both places again which I really enjoyed. St. Petersburg had Fort Desoto, a nature area whose name I forget, and the Dali museum. Cedar Key was like going back to the 50s. It is 25 miles across swampland near the mouth of the Suwannee River. Marcia and I hired a boat and had a whole day to ourselves on an island off shore with no other people. It was quite a remarkable place. I don't know if it is still undeveloped, but it was then!

U.S. Virgin Islands

In 1990 I and eleven other 12 step friends chartered the schooner Harvey Gamage and sailed around the Virgin Islands for ten days. We slept on the deck mostly and had meetings at night. We sailed each day to where we collectively decided we wanted to go and dropped anchor for the night wherever we chose. We visited St. Thomas, Saint John, Tortola, Treasure Island, and Joss Van Dyke as I remember. It was one of the most enjoyable vacations I ever took!

Trip west to Idaho, Washington, and British Columbia

In 1992, Rich B. and I drove Brenda P.'s car from Newburyport to Spokane, Washington where she had moved. I drove with Rich to Vancouver, BC where we stayed on a houseboat owned by friends of his. Then I drove alone through Washington, Oregon and Idaho revisiting places I had first seen when I lived in Idaho. I particularly remember Golden, Washington as a very interesting place. The first time I saw it was drunk in 1979 with a Basque friend named Steve. We were driving to the coast to go salmon fishing and suddenly in the middle of nowhere Stonehenge appeared! You can imagine our disbelief! It turns out that it was a 3/4 size model of Stonehenge as it was originally built. It was built by a fellow named Sam Hill and contributed in part, no doubt, to the expression "What in the Sam Hill??" Golden has a Sam Hill museum and a fabulous observatory open to the public. I drove up there on a rainy night, disappointed and not expecting to see much. Suddenly the sky cleared, and as I was the only guest that night, I had complete use of the telescope for two hours. It was awesome!

On this trip I also visited the White Cloud battleground and the grave of Chief Joseph of the Nez pierce, one of my personal heroes. I spent three great days with Brenda in Coeur d'Alene, ID, Coleville, WA, and Spokane. Rich and I had visited many of the great western sites on the way including Yellowstone, the Badlands, the Black Hills, the Grand Tetons, and the Great Horn Mountains. It was another wonderful trip. We flew back from Seattle, WA.

Yes, I worked during this time, but as I look back on my life, it isn't the work I remember but the travels and people. Vinette, who I mentioned earlier, and who is still a friend today, once had a clothing line named after her. And she eventually closed it to focus on more creative fine art. She said, correctly I believe, "I am so much more than just a dress label!"

1993 -1994 Plum Island

These were the year's I first got involved on-line. I was one of the first 350,000 members of AOL. I helped start 12 step programs on-line, was a host in the People Connection of AOL, maintained an on-line presence for Bird Watcher's Digest, and helped found the AOL Birders Forum. I helped plan the Online Intergroup demonstration for the AA International Convention in San Diego in 1995. This was before there was a World Wide Web and before match.com and other on-line dating. Nevertheless, I met Carol (not her real name) on-line and we had a long-distance relationship.

Carol was a physician on the west coast. After six months we met in Tucson, Az. Later she visited me in Massachusetts and Alex and I visited her on the West Coast. I cannot remember how it came up, but I was really impressed because although she had a very nice home in a very nice suburb, she grew vegetables and wildflowers in her front yard instead of having a front lawn.

We dated for over a year, but the relationship eventually ended because she was content with a "boyfriend in a box" available when desired but not intrusive at other times and I wanted a more involved relationship. Ironically, today I think I understand the desire she had for an intimate relationship but an independent life.

I belonged to a Men's Group which met once a week. AA, bird watching, and genealogy were my passions. I spent every other weekend with Alex and her best friend Carly. I bought my House on Plum Island with my mother's help. I built the downstairs apartment with my friend Bill who moved in with his wife Susan when it was done. Bill and I studied Astrology and became astrologers with the help of a computer program and did horoscopes for a fee. I was quite good at this although not a true believer!

Every Wednesday I would have dinner at the Starboard Galley with friends (The House Special was steak tips and shrimp). I wrote articles for the Plum Island Pages on Nature and a few other articles for local Newspapers. I really enjoyed writing, although I never made much money at it.

After I broke up with Carol in 1994, I quit smoking and started a local meeting to help others quit. That was the hardest thing I ever did, quitting smoking! Harder than giving up alcohol, but I haven' t smoked since. On Friday nights daughter Alex and her best friend Carly and I would have dinner at the Anna Jacques Hospital cafeteria and then they would go to my meeting with me. I don't know if it helped any of the other attendees, but it certainly helped me through that difficult process! I think those kids were a great motivator for me! And I am very grateful at my current age to have healthy lungs as I get older!

I had been planning to move to the West Coast and live with Carol, so I announced I was leaving CTI in Lowell and trained my replacement. Neither Carol nor Betsy thought it was a good idea for me to move away from Alex and they were right about that! Carol and I broke up. As a result, I became unemployed for several months and went to work for my neighbor who had opened a bird watching supply and gift shop. One day a fellow came in to buy bird seed. I had known him a few years earlier when I had worked for the State. He was the CFO of LEO, Inc. a human service agency in Lynn, MA. He knew my computer skills, so he offered me a part time job. This would eventually turn into a full-time job as Information Services Director for fifteen years for LEO, Inc. in Lynn.

San Diego, CA

The big event for me in 1995 was an International Convention in San Diego, CA. The whole thing was rather miraculous for me.

I had been involved in arranging the first demonstration of 12 step recovery On-Line at the Convention. We set up several computers in a suite in one of the hotels and had live on-line meetings 24 hours a day for people who couldn't come to San Diego but did belong to one of the three big commercial on-line services (AOL, CompuServe, and Delphi). This was before the Internet.

Rooms are assigned by lottery at such conventions, but I had booked a luxury suite a year in advance with a fellow from Australia. He sent me half the money but said he couldn't make it after-all, but I could keep the money. I then advertised that I had space on-line and got emails from several interested people. I ended up selling three more beds in the suite. Basically, I paid for my whole trip to San Diego this way including hotel, airfare, and food and a rental car.

My roommates turned out to be a great bunch of guys from New York and California. We drank Starbucks Sumatra coffee every morning (Starbucks was still a west coast chain), went to the San Diego Zoo, and Hotel Coronado. One day I took the car and went bird watching near the Mexican border where

I was buzzed by US immigration helicopters. I also ventured into the mountains just east of San Diego. Some nights I worked the on-line meetings at another hotel.

This was the biggest (and best behaved according to local papers) convention in San Diego history. There were 65,000 attendees. One night we filled the Jack Murphy Stadium (home of the San Diego Padres). Every restaurant and coffee shop downtown and along the beach were filled with convention attendees! The only local business that suffered were the bars! It was fabulous!

Ipswich MA and Maine

I worked that summer for an architect in Ipswich, MA. His specialty was testifying as an expert witness at trials and I prepared the testimony for him. I got fired after three months which was just as well. I don't think my heart was in the job, preparing testimony to defeat little old ladies suing churches for falls or to defend landlords being sued for unsafe living conditions. Sometimes, I took a camera to the scene of an accident and took pictures to back up the story of whoever was paying us. I got a bad taste for lawyers then and in my later divorces!

I met Deidre and she became my tenant on Plum Island and then my wife. We got married in a Quaker Service at the Meeting House in

Amesbury. A picture of Deidre picking flowers for her wedding was on the front page of the local paper. I remember as we drove to the wedding Alex and Carly were singing an Alanis Morrissette song, "it's like rain on your wedding day." I think it was rainy although the sun came out later. We had the reception under a tent on the front lawn of the Meeting House. I think everyone had a good time dancing the Macarena and the Electric Slide. The cake was beautiful. In what is apparently a Portuguese tradition, the kids beat a bat on a piñata that looked like a bride to get candy out of it. This didn't sit too well with some of the Quakers present.

We had a very nice honeymoon in Maine including stops in Kennebunkport, the Blue Hills, and Bar Harbor. Our life situations and hopes were different though. Deidre had two kids who were grown up and on their own. My daughter was ten. Deidre hated her job as a teacher and wanted to move to Maine and open a B&B. I was unemployed but I wanted to find a job locally and stay on Plum Island. Deidre moved to Maine and I stayed on Plum Island and found a job in Lynn. We got divorced using a mediator instead of opposing lawyers and went to court with a mutually agreed settlement.

I thought the agreement was fair. Some years later Deidre told me she thought she got ripped off. A lawyer once told me that a good divorce is a divorce in which nobody is happy because that means

Figure 76 Ed at Wedding of Deidre and Ed 1996

the divorce was fair. Deidre had introduced me to the Society of Friends which has become a big part of my life although I don't believe she kept attending for more than a couple of years in Maine.

1997 -1998

I was working in Lynn and that is when I went to Washington, DC for Head Start Information System Training with June (my future wife), Nancy and Joanne. We all had a good time seeing the sites of DC and flying in and out of Dulles Airport. Our actual training was in Rockville, MD and we stayed at a hotel that had pretty good appetizers at 5 PM.

Joanne and Nancy who both worked for me had a huge fight outside the White House. Joanne left after a couple of years, but Nancy and I worked together for over 10 years. Her son, Alexander, also the same age as my Alex, is a Doctor today! I feel good about the fact that Nancy who was a Head Start Mom, and Alexander who was a Head Start kid, have made a life for themselves! Joanne also had a rough life and I still get reference requests from her from time to time. Nancy also had a daughter Kaisha and when Kaisha had a baby Nancy became a grandmother.

1998 was the year Deidre and I got divorced. She moved to Maine and I stayed in Newburyport. I met June at a twelve step meeting and went to her birthday party on the beach at Plum Island where it turned out we had some mutual friends that thought we would make a great couple. June was from Norwich, England and her sister and brother-in-law from Newcastle, UK were visiting at the time and they encouraged us as well.

During this time, I attended many twelve step meetings and spent time mostly with people in recovery programs. My parents were not alcoholics, but I found a lot of discussion there helpful. I concluded that while the disease may have skipped a generation or two, many of the dysfunctional family symptoms seemed to be present in my life. My later genealogical research confirmed my hunch! I also became a regular member of the Amesbury Friends Meeting and was Building Clerk there.

June and I went to some work conferences in places like Hyannis, Boston, and Northampton during these years. I continued to be involved with the Low-Income Energy Assistance Program in Massachusetts although now from an Information Technology perspective rather than a program perspective.

It was also about this time that I started attending New England Yearly meeting annual sessions in Smithfield, RI for a week each August. These sessions were held one year at Wheaton College and one year at Stonehill College but most often they were at Bryant College (later University). In more recent years they have been held at Castleton University in Vermont.

England

This period was dominated by my marriage to June and trips to England to visit her family in Norwich. I do remember we also flew to Newcastle via Amsterdam which seems to be crazy but was the quickest and cheaper way to get there rather than going through London. June found my genealogy hunting interesting or at least she tolerated it kindly, so I was able to find several early Newbury families in East Anglia and Suffolk where they emigrated from to the US.

1999 was quite a New Year's Eve. June and I came back from England with a terrible flu on December 30. This was the year of Y2K and I was on stand-by for work in case a disaster happened. I really began to have problems with my boss after he dismissed the problem on January 3 saying, "See nothing happened." I was upset because I had chosen to take what simple precautions that I could and not spend $1,000s like many companies on consultants and disaster plans. Yeah, there was no disaster and we didn't lose much money because of tough decisions I made not knowing what was going to happen. Anyway, unlike Prince, I didn't get to party like it was 1999!

Lebanon, NH

June and I spent three Christmases during this time at the Shaker Great Stone House on Mascoma Lake near Lebanon, NH. One year we took a walk on the solidly frozen Lake with Peter and Loretta Land. The ice was so clear you could see fish swimming below. It was spectacular! In other years my Taggart cousins joined us for a Wood Family reunion and my mother joined us for Christmas at the Great Stone House.

My friends Saul Chadis, Peter Land and I climbed Mt. Adams about this time and I broke my median cruciate ligament near the summit. That resulted in a very painful night in an AMC hut with a bag of frozen peas on my knee, and excruciating descent the next day and ended my mountain climbing days.

Saul taught me the trick of double tying my hiking boot shoelaces which I later used many times in the Northeast and Europe.

Peter and I had differing political views. Nevertheless, he graciously let me stay at his house while I was campaigning for John Kerry in New Hampshire.

Carly, Alex, Deidre and I once hiked to the Lake in the Clouds AMC camp. The view of the stars at night was indescribable and I woke the girls up to see it!

On the death date of John Greenleaf Whittier, Peter and I and a few other friends climbed Mt. Moosilauke as Lucy Larcom, one of my favorite poets, had done on the day he died.

Travels

I have walked many trails whenever I get the chance. For examples, I have walked Walden Woods, the Wang Institute Grounds, Drumlin Farm, Arcadia, Purgatory Chasm, The Flume, The Camino Santiago, Talbot Mt., Mt. Tom, Mt. Holyoke, Yellowstone, the Salisbury Rail Trail and Hellcat swamp at the Parker River NWR.

Figure 78 Saul and Ed on Mt Adams

Figure 77 Ed and Peter on Mt. Washington

I met Donald McDonald Dickinson Thurber in 1999. He was Gerrish Thurber's second cousin. One of the more interesting people I have had the chance to know. Donald was very interested in family history and wrote to me after seeing some of my research online. He lived in Grosse Pointe, Michigan. I figured he was a wealthy Republican, but I wrote him a pretty honest email about my being a liberal and in recovery and a Quaker.

Well he was wealthy, but he turned out to be a liberal Democrat as well. He was JFKs roommate at Harvard University and helped, as Chairman of the Democratic State Committee bring Michigan into JFKs column He was CEO of Blue Cross/Blue Shield of Michigan, Chairman of the Trustees of the University of Michigan, and an Overseer (Trustee) of Harvard. His doctor was in Boston and he came twice a year to Boston for his medical care.

It was in 1999 that Donald took Marggie, myself, my daughter Alex, and her friend Carly to the Harvard Club for dinner and the fourth of July fireworks. He also took me to Kingston, NH to the homestead of Josiah Bartlett (our close relation who signed the Declaration of Independence and introduced me to Josiah's descendant who lives there Ruth Bartlett Semple Albert. Ruth and her husband Dale and I have remained friends ever since.

One afternoon Donald Thurber had his limousine and chauffer drop him off to visit a friend in East Gloucester and then turned the limo and driver over to us for the rest of the day. I confess that I had the driver take us to a restaurant owned by my ex-wife Deidre's sister in Essex, MA for seafood. Donald died the next year while I was walking on the property of our mutual ancestor Joseph Gerrish in Newbury, now called Great Meadows Farm.

Our shared love of genealogy made us almost instant close friends, even if briefly. Donald was Episcopalian but he seemed to genuinely enjoy visiting our Quaker Meeting House in Amesbury. He was a strong supporter of the Sons and Daughters of the First Settlers of Newbury which I become President of in later years. I think I learned from knowing him that not all rich guys are bad!

2000 was the year that both Donald Thurber and Gerrish Thurber died. It was at Gerrish Thurber's memorial service that I met Diane King-Taggart and Bill Taggart. It was also the last time I saw Ed Thurber and his family. I can't believe that was so long ago either! I have seen the Taggarts almost every year since and I look forward to it!

Donald Thurber: *Helped save Orchestra Hall*

Figure 79 Donald McDonald Dickinson Thurber

Chapter XX 2001 - 2002

Scotland

2001 was the year I turned 50 and visited Scotland as had my grandfather and father before me in their 50th year. I went with June and we met Marggie in Edinburgh after a visit with June's sister in Newcastle. June went back to Newcastle and Marggie and I took a train north. We visited Cousin Grace Brimlow in Kelso and the Catto family in Aberdeen. We visited Udny, the village of our great great grandfather George Mair, "old Logie," who lived until age 100 and married two sisters. We were accompanied to Udny by our cousin Peter Catto. I was now interested in genealogy and had a great time visiting family graves, family homes, and organizations like the Aberdeen Genealogical Society. I thoroughly enjoyed this trip and would love to go back to Scotland someday!

Figure 80 Aberdeen, Scotland

June became pregnant this year which was unexpected. She later had a miscarriage, also unexpected. This was devastating to her and hard on me, but I was quietly relieved. Alex did not like the idea of having a baby sister at all.

Lebanon, NH

Diane, Barbara, and Cindy Taggart and (baby Abby) came to the Wood Family Reunion in Lebanon, ME with Marggie and me. We ended up in the middle a wedding party which had moved inside because of rain at the Great Stone House at the Shaker Village where we stayed. Abby won the youngest attender award at the reunion and I later became President of the Family Association for three years. This is the NH family of Sarah Augusta Wood, Samuel Wood, Joseph Wood Jr. (a centenarian), and Joseph Wood Sr. a founding father of Lebanon. The Woods came to the Upper Valley area of NH through Charlestown, MA, Rowley, MA, and Mansfield, CT. Rowley, MA is the next town to Newbury where I

Figure 81 Lebanon, NH

live. I visited the USS Constitution which is berthed in Charlestown and the Bunker Hill Monument. I also visited The University of Connecticut in the village of Storrs in Mansfield, CT.

Cancer (Melanoma)

2002 was the year I had cancer (melanoma) and June and I got married while I was sick. My treatment involved two surgeries, trips to Boston for chemo every day for one month, and a stay of one week in the hospital in Boston after I had an experience something like a stroke where I could not talk for a few hours. For the rest of the year I had to inject myself with interferon three times a week. Interferon makes you feel like you have the flu, so it was quite an unpleasant experience, but I survived which, of course, made it all worthwhile to me! June coordinated rides to Boston for me and my care at the hospital. I will always be grateful for that kindness.

Our wedding was a Quaker ceremony which was well attended, and we took a honeymoon to Maine. I recently was looking at some pictures from that trip including a couple where I assisted in banding and releasing warblers near Wells, ME. We stayed at the Cliff House in Ogunquit, ME which has a spectacular view of the Ocean and is a great sea bird watching spot. It also has a spa which we indulged in. The doctors at Tufts New England Medical Center had allowed me to go off medication for ten days so I could enjoy the wedding and honeymoon.

Figure 82 Tufts New England Medical Center Boston, MA

Chapter XXI Newbury, MA 2003 - 2004

I recovered from the melanoma. Around Christmas of 2003 June got quite manic which I didn't recognize at the time. I thought she was just happy and full of energy. However, the following year she became depressed and suicidal. She was hospitalized several times, first in Portsmouth, NH and later at Maclean Hospital, MA. I spent several nights in Waltham, MA at two or three hotels so I could visit her. During one of her rare stays at home we got her a cockapoo named Maisy who then accompanied me on my trips to Waltham to visit June. I could see that Maisy really brightened up the day for June and her fellow patients who came out during smoke breaks to see her.

I attended several therapy sessions with June both at the hospital and at home. I paid all June's bills recording them on a spreadsheet which I would take to the hospital to show June. She would then reimburse me from her checking account. When her custom-made wedding, ring was stolen I returned to the Jeweler and had another one made.

When nothing else seemed to work, June agreed to Electric Shock treatments to all of which I accompanied her. The result of the ECT was that June apparently lost her short-term memory.

To the complete surprise of myself and our mutual marriage therapist back in Newburyport, June announced one evening that she wanted a divorce and ask the therapist to keep me in the office until she could safely get away. In her opening statement before the judge in our divorce hearing June's high-priced Boston lawyer declared that June had supported me through my cancer but that I hadn't lifted a finger to help her during her time of trouble. I was really very angry and declared that while the former was true, the latter was patently false.

At another point, June declared that I had stolen the money for the wedding ring from her. This really hurt because I had gone out of my way and spent my own money to have her lost custom-made ring

Figure 83 Ed in Florida during marriage to June

replaced. Even her own lawyer seemed surprised at that statement. In the end my lawyer said to give her whatever she wanted and be glad she was going to disappear from my life. To sum up, after I had lived in my house for twenty years and she had lived there two she walked away at the peak of the housing market with 50% of the equity in my house but I got the title back and still live there. However, the real estate market collapsed soon after this while my daughter was still in college, June also tried to get half the money I had set aside for Alex's education but was not successful in this matter. This episode has made my life much more difficult, but as my lawyer suggested it is wonderful to have my liberty back. It was also a lesson in acceptance and living one day at a time.

Chapter XXII Lynn, MA 2005 - 2006

I was single during this time and dated a few times through match.com. I have found that by this age (50s) most people who are well adjusted for marriage are already married, content, and unavailable. So, that leaves those of us who are carrying some baggage, often from unsuccessful marriages. It has taken me awhile to conclude this and I had not by 2005. That is not to say that all unmarried people are uninteresting or unattractive. However, looking for a lifetime mate among people who have already been down that road and found it difficult is challenging! I believe widows are the most likely good partners at age 50.

I corresponded with maybe a dozen women and I think I went on actual dates six times. The one incident I remember most clearly was somewhat unpleasant. The woman I saw perhaps three times was a lawyer from central Massachusetts. She spent a lot of time complaining about how unfairly her family treated her. On the third date she came to Newburyport and I took her to dinner. When we returned to my house, she said "OK, let's go" and headed for the bedroom. Maybe this is the same experience many women have, but I was appalled and said that I wasn't ready for that. She exploded with anger, saying she hadn't driven all this way just for dinner and threw money at me saying that she was sorry she had troubled me and taken my money, hopped in her car, and drove off. Then she wrote a letter to match.com saying I falsely advertised that I was "available". Match.com contacted me and accepted my explanation and I was not banned!

Lynn, MA

I continued to work at LEO in Lynn and commute by train. It was during this time that I entered a photo contest in Lynn and won a ribbon and had my picture displayed at the Historical Park Museum. I did some research at the local historical society on

LEO Building Lynn, MA

Figure 84 LEO Lynn, MA

Quakers in Lynn. They were once a big presence in the city but died out and sold their property to the African Methodist Episcopal Church. Two cemeteries remain for the "old lights" and the "new lights". Two apartment buildings remain called Haverford and Earlham across the street from where three of us present day Quakers worked on Broad Street in Lynn.

Nova Scotia

June and I took a ferry trip to Nova Scotia for the marriage of my friends Gerry Corcoran and Deanne Horangic. While there we did some Gerrish family genealogical research and bird watching. It is a beautiful place, to which, unfortunately, I have never returned.

Lynn, MA

Lubbock, Texas

I took a trip to Lubbock, Texas with my assistant Nancy and her daughter Kaisha. Lubbock was an amazingly interesting place as was the campus of Texas Tech University. We saw a prairie dog town, the Western Texas Hall of Fame (Buddy Holly), a windmill museum and a museum rather like a Texas Sturbridge Village.

I took some great pictures in and around Lubbock. We also drove to Roswell, NM and Carlsbad Cavern and stopped at a local winery where a country band was playing. The Dallas Cowboys and the Texas Tech Red Riders were very popular in that area! We were there for classes at Texas Tech on the Head Start Federal Information System which we were using at LEO.

Figure 85 Windmill Museum Lubbock, TX

Figure 86 Quaker Canvass Poster

Amesbury, MA

These were the years I was Clerk (president) of the Amesbury Monthly Meeting of Friends, President of the Wood Family Association of New Hampshire, and Secretary of the Amesbury Council of Churches. I also appeared monthly as a panelist on the local cable show "Faith Matters". I was once approached by a stranger at the Lynn train station who said, "Hey aren't you Ed that Quaker fellow I saw on TV" Kevin has been a member of our Meeting in Amesbury ever since. I imagine serving like this is in my genes. My father was on 30 Committees when he died! My mother was President of the Northampton League of Women

Voters at one point and on the Alumni Council of Mary Baldwin College in Virginia. My sister had been involved with the historical town of Wethersfield, CT, the Hartford Athenaeum, the Harriet Beecher Stowe house, and St. James Episcopal Church she attends in West Hartford, CT.

In 2006 I gave a talk about the "Faith of Josiah Bartlett" at the Rocky Hill Meeting House, (built in 1785) in Amesbury, MA. It is a wonderful old Meeting House and I was fortunate to have the opportunity to speak from the two-story pulpit with a sounding board. The Meeting House has box pews, original marbleized paint on its interior pillars, and graffiti from the 19th century. Afterward I had dinner with Ruth and Dale Albert. Ruth is a direct descendant of Josiah Bartlett and lived in his house in Kingston, NH. Josiah was the first person to sign the Declaration of Independence after John Hancock and is a first cousin several times removed of myself and my cousins! The last appearance of the name in our family that I am aware of was Mary Bartlett Gerrish Thurber Wood, the grandmother of Dr. Samuel Wood Thurber, husband of Bertha Fisk.

Figure 87 Josiah Bartlett, NH Signer of Declaration of Independence (courtesy of Ruth Albert)

New York

Alex was in college at Adelphi University during this time and I visited her in Garden City Long Island a few times. She was very thoughtful in finding Quaker Meetings to attend and I was very happy when we visited the Jericho Meeting and found the grave of Elias Hicks. Elias was the namesake of the Hicksite Quakers who broke away from the Orthodox Quakers in the 19th century. His family name was incorporated into the name of the town Hicksville, NY and I would not be surprised if the term "hicks" came from them as well since at that time Long Island was very rural and the Hicksite movement basically split rural Quakers from Philadelphia city Quakers. Elias Hicks was also the first cousin of the Newtown, PA painter Edward Hicks who painted a series of well-known pictures of a lamb and a lion lying down together.

I also took the ferries from CT and saw other parts of Long Island on these trips including visiting my prep school friend Dan in Montauk.

Alex brought culture back into my life during my visits to see her. I stayed in New York City hotels and visited the Today show. Guests that I saw there included Lionel Richie, Rhianna, and the girl who played Little Miss Sunshine

England

During the year 2006 I also took a trip to England with a delegation of Episcopalians from Amesbury, MA to Amesbury, Wiltshire, England. Annie Tunstall, Richard Gale, and I represented Quakers and attended Quaker meeting in the shadow of Salisbury, Cathedral. We also visited Glastonbury, Avesbury, Stonehenge, and a Quaker Cemetery on the property of Madonna in Wiltshire.

Amesbury, MA and New York City

While Alex was at Adelphi University in Garden City, NY (Long Island) from 2004 until 2008, I visited again MOMA, the Natural History Museum, Central Park, and the Metropolitan Museum of Art. I also attended concerts by Paul McCartney and Ringo Starr and the play Wicked as well as a play in which Will Farrell played George W. Bush. I visited the Today Show seeing Katy Couric, Natalie Morales, Matt Lauer, Al Roker, as well as chatting with Meredith Vieira briefly about the Boston Red Sox.

Figure 88 Will Farrell plays George W. Bush

Chapter XXIII Newbury, MA Metro West, Long Island, Spain 2007 - 2008

These were the years when I met the woman, I would spend the next ten years with, and Alex graduated from Adelphi. I signed up for Holiday Inn's frequent guest program and always stayed at a Holiday Inn when visiting Alex. By the time my daughter graduated I had enough points to stay at the Inn for free.

The speaker at Alex's graduation at the Nassau Coliseum was Senator Chuck Schumer. I attended with my ex-wife Betsy and her family and we all got along well although I remember Alex being somewhat stressed out dealing with all of us at the same time.

My closest companion from 2007-2017 prefers to remain unidentified. My first date with her was at the Museum of Fine Arts in Boston. I thought how lucky I was to have met such a beautiful and intelligent woman. I still think that although we broke up several years ago. She lived west of Boston and grew up in Asia. I learned a lot about Chinese culture and Boston from her.

I planted a garden at her house and spent most weekends there.

My favorite drive to and from her house took me past Walden and through the Lexington and Concord battle road. I enjoyed visiting the sites of Concord including Authors' Ridge in the cemetery. I discovered in my genealogy research that I am distantly related to several of the transcendentalist authors from Concord.

In 2008 we took our first trip to Spain, flying on British Air through London. We spent most of our time in Andalusia. We stayed at the Alhambra in Granada, but my favorite places were the Mosque in Cordoba and the town of Ronda. Ronda is split in two by a deep chasm spanned by a high arched bridge. We stayed at the Dom Jose hotel perched on the side of the chasm and it was the most romantic room I have ever stayed in. Ronda is the home of many British ex-pats and Spain's first bull ring. I have never gone to a bull fight and I believe many persons were hurled into the chasm in Ronda during the civil war in Spain.

In its earlier history Ronda was the seat of a Muslim caliphate and the ruler's palace still may be toured. Ronda is not too distant from the rock of Gibraltar and the Mediterranean coast, both of which we visited.

Figure 90 Cordoba, Spain

Figure 89 Consuegra, Spain

Figure 91 Segovia, Spain

Figure 92 Ronda, Spain

Chapter XXIV Newbury, MA and Hartford, CT 2009-2011

My mother died in 2010 in February. In March of 2010 I left my job at LEO Inc. in Lynn, MA and spent several months straightening out my mother's affairs. My relationship in Metro west continued and I became Treasurer of the New England Yearly Meeting of Friends. I travelled to Worcester, MA to the office of NEYM once a week and became quite active in the affairs of New England Quakers.

I went to Spain each summer. My travels took me to many of the same locales and some new ones such as the Basque country of Northern Spain, the northern kingdoms of Galicia, and Asturias. I spent time on the Camino de Santiago and in Santiago de Compostela. One of my favorite memories is staying in Burgos with a view of the cathedral and fireworks right outside the window.

I was also in Sevilla the night that Spain won the world cup and it seemed the whole city was up all night celebrating and waving flags.

I also had the opportunity to take interesting trips to South Bend, IN and Washington, DC. On the trip to Indiana I was surprised to find the Cleveland, Ohio airport is in Kentucky!

Jean Lois Baum Mair (April 9, 2009 - February 24, 2010)

My mother was born in Lakewood NJ, the daughter of Granville Baum (1893 -1928) and Katheryn Conover (1893-1981). The Baums are from the Virginia Beach, VA/Cape Hatteras, NC area and we believe migrated from the Palatinate region between France and Germany in the 18th century. The Conover's original family name was Van Kouwenhoven and they came to New Amsterdam in the 17th century. My mother's father died when she was nine years old and her single mother raised her by supporting herself as a schoolteacher, eventually settling in Princeton, NJ. Many summers were spent in the Norfolk, Virginia area with relatives including the Rev. Herman Baum and his wife Lota Leigh. As I child I attended some Baum family reunions in Virginia and met some of my southern cousins.

My mother had some sort of mental illness not formally diagnosed during her lifetime as far as I know. She was very intelligent and narcissistic. I now realize she had a frustrating life being married to a well-respected professor at a woman's' college. She held several administrative and clerical jobs at Smith College in the library, Day School, plant house and art museum. She also achieved three master's degrees in education, library science and art history.

She was a President of the League of Women Voters, A member of the Alumni Council of Mary Baldwin College, and active in the P.E.O. sorority and the Monday Afternoon Women's Club.

After my father died, she lived in the family home and then an apartment in Northampton, and finally moved to the Duncaster Community in Bloomfield, CT for the last 25 years of her life.

Figure 93 Jean Baum Mair and Angus the cat

My sister and I managed to work together to have memorial services for my mother in Hartford and Ewing, NJ. Uncle David presided over the Ewing ceremony by cell phone from Michigan. My Taggart cousins came across the Delaware River from Pennsylvania to the service in Ewing, NJ. That meant a lot to me.

At this time, I purchased gravestones for my mother and myself from her estate. At the time, Marggie didn't want one, thinking she would be buried with my father in Valhalla, NY. Shortly before she died, she changed her mind and I had a memorial to my Dad added to my mother's gravestone and purchased a gravestone for Marggie.

Someday we will all be together in Ewing.

Salisbury, Cathedral, England

Chapter XXV Newbury, MA 2012-2013

Figure 94 Unitarian Church Steeple Repair Newburyport, MA

Plum Island 2010s

From 2012 until 2018 I worked as the part time Sexton of the First Religious Society. At lunchtime, I usually went to Anchor Pizza and visited my daughter Alex at the frozen yogurt store where she worked. I also worked at the Community Supported Agriculture (CSA) farm Arrowhead on Friday mornings. I didn't get paid but received a weekly share of the week's fresh produce.

As part of my responsibilities as Treasurer of NEYM I attended bi-monthly meetings of the NEYM Board of Managers of pooled funds. For these meetings I took the train to Boston and had lunch at the Harvard Club. This is one of four Boards I sat on. The others were The Permanent Board of NEYM, the Friends Mutual Health Group in Philadelphia, and the Sons & Daughters of the First Settlers of Newbury. With my work at the UU Church and the Friends I felt rather like I had returned home to the roots of my branch of our family. Many of my ancestors, as well as my grandfather and uncle were ministers.

On December 21, 2012 the world did not end! This was an obvious reference for people in 2012 to the supposed end of the Mayan Calendar. It is perhaps not so clear if you are reading this many years later!

On New Year's Day 2013 I went to West Newton to see Lincoln at the movies. A good movie I thought. Amazing how the two national parties have switched roles since then. Dinner that night was at an Indian restaurant in Waltham.

The work on the farm in winter was often greenhouse repairs. I remember John getting all the greenhouse generators working and putting snowplows on the farm trucks. I saw a Red-tailed hawk sitting nearby and then flying off into the snow. That is one of my favorite images ever! A Red-tailed Hawk flying in the snow. There is a painting of this image by Robert Altman which is one of my favorites.

I spent a night at Woolman Hill, the Quaker Retreat Center in Deerfield, MA. As Treasurer of the New England Yearly Meeting (NEYM) I was on the Coordinating and Advisory Committee for NEYM along with the Presiding Clerk, Clerk of Permanent Board, Clerk of Ministry and Counsel, and Yearly Meeting Secretary. At the time, the people holding these positions were Jackie S., Holly B., Margaret C., and Noah M. In the corporate world we would probably be called the Executive Committee of the Board of Directors or the corporate officers. I was a member of this group for three years. This was a particularly good group and we had good retreat together.

I again travelled in Spain in the summer both years and I attended the annual sessions of New England Yearly Meeting of Friends. I attended these Sessions and the generic 12 step meeting at Sessions every year for 20 years. Most of these years I volunteered as a golf cart shuttle driver at night to transport elderly and disabled people around the Campus. This activity allowed me to become quite familiar with the various campuses where Sessions were held: Bryant University in Smithfield, RI, Stoneham College in Stoneham, MA, Wheaton College in Norwood, MA, and Castleton University in Vermont.

As I made my weekly trips to Worcester, MA in my capacity of Treasurer of the New England Yearly Meeting of Friends, I usually stopped at a Dunkin Donuts for my weekly Big n Toasty sandwich!

In 2013 I began a five-year journey as a part time sexton at the First Religious Society UU of Newburyport. It felt right working in a church as my grandfather and grandmother Mair had done in New Jersey in the 1950s and1960s. One Sunday I gave the sermon at the First Religious Society on being a Quaker in the 21st century. With a little assistance from the Minister, Harold Babcock,

Plum Island 2010s

I conducted the service at the Unitarian church doing all the readings and giving the sermon. The UU Church has a raised pulpit and although I was describing Quakers and what we believe, I had the feeling of being Leo DiCaprio standing on the bow of the Titanic! One of the parishioners who greeted me was a man whom I met 50 years ago as a child in Northampton, MA. Another was a woman I dated about six years ago. Others were people I have met over the years in Newburyport and many, of course, were strangers who seemed interested in what I had to stay.

Too often in my life I have seen non-profits morph into corporate beings whose primary goal becomes to perpetuate themselves rather than fulfill their original mission. These two groups, Unitarians and Quakers seem to realize that sometimes the world changes, sometimes real needs are met, and it is time to "lay down" an institution and put resources towards more contemporary goals.

On Christmas morning 2013, Brian Fisk (Pliny Fisk's grandson) called and said he and his mother Cynthia wouldn't be able to have lunch with us because he had a bad case of the flu. This worked out fine. My sister Marggie came over from the motel in Gloucester where she was staying, and we went to a Chinese Restaurant (Szechuan Taste) for lunch. I also gave her a tour of the 1801 First Religious Society Church where I was Sexton.

We had dinner with Alex (my daughter) and Betsy (her mom and my ex-wife). Alex posted on Facebook that it was the first time she had been able spend Christmas with both her parents since 1988. Sorry about that Alex, but I certainly enjoyed this Christmas!

In 2013, I attended a meeting of the Coordinating and Advisory Committee of NEYM (the Executive Committee of the Permanent Board) of which I was now the most senior member, both in age and in length of being on the Committee.

The Journey Not the Destination

I believe I set the world record for the number of Unitarian Churches visited and photographed in three hours (seven). This dubious achievement was sparked by my need to return to Newburyport for a memorial service one Sunday afternoon and my recollection that I had passed many churches on this drive in the past. Smart phones with cameras help too. The churches photographed were South Natick, Wayland, Concord, Carlisle, Chelmsford, North Andover, and Newburyport. In N. Andover I made a quick detour to the Academy Street burial grounds and visited the memorial stones to ancestors Richard Swan, Job Tyler, and Ann Dudley Bradstreet.

In March of 2013 there was a surprise snowstorm that dumped over a foot of snow on Plum Island and caused serious beach erosion. Three houses fell into the ocean and I could see two of them from my house. The story was on the National News as well as the Boston news. I had to show my Driver's ID to get home. There were National Guard troops guarding the beach.

Later in March 2013, I went to Portland, ME. I celebrated my 62nd birthday at a Korean Restaurant in Portland. The next day I ate two great seafood meals at the Cape Neddick Lobster Pound in York, ME and Fishbones in Chelmsford, MA. I got to the beach for the first time after the recent storms and took some pictures which I posted on Facebook.

Two turkeys walked across the backyard one day. It is strange how common they are now compared to when I was a kid when they were so rare. I think it is because of the reforestation that has taken place in Massachusetts as agricultural lands became abandoned. In April one finds many stone walls deep in the woods before all the plants have leaves. The first crocus plants bloom, the grackles have returned to the woods, the Canada geese are flying south, and the snow is gone. Spring has come finally!

After the Boston Marathon bombing, Boston and surrounding communities were on lock down as the hunt for the bombers intensified. One was killed and several hours later another was captured injured in Watertown. The suspects were Chechen brothers 26 and 19. I was happy to get away to western Mass. where I attended a Quaker Coordinating and Advisory Committee Meeting in Greenfield. I spent the night in the John Greenleaf Whittier room of the Poetry Ridge B&B. It was expensive and quite beautiful, and I was the only guest.

I attended a Funding Our Vision Workshop at the Mt. Toby Friends Meeting in Leveret, MA. I had an early dinner with two Quaker Friends at the Route 9 diner in Amherst. It was strange driving the UMASS campus nearly 40 years since I was a graduate student attending there. The campus appears much larger with many more buildings and "very young" students everywhere in town!
I drove back through Ware and Palmer on Route 32 by the Quabbin Reservoir.

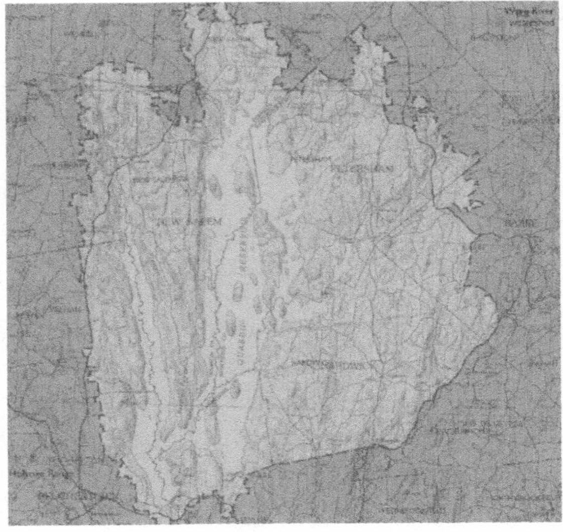

The Quabbin reservoir in West Central Massachusetts drowned six towns but has become a wonderful bird and wildlife refuge. It was the first place in MA where Turkeys and Eagles returned after DDT

Figure 95 Quabbin Reservoir Ware, MA

Chapter XXVI Newbury, MA 2014

White Privilege

I had a dream one night. The subject was white privilege, so it was probably actually a letter from my subconscious since this is frequent concern among Quakers. Well, yes, our family clearly fits into that group of people who have been privileged for 300 years. Some of my ancestors were involved in slaughtering the Pequot tribe in Rhode Island and stripping Quaker women to the waist, tying them to carts, and marching them from town to town for public whippings. Samuel Sewall was a judge at the Salem witch trials, Thomas Fisk was foreman on the jury that sentenced the witches to be hanged.

Samuel Sewall was the only principle character in the witch trials to admit he was wrong and publicly apologize and he was the first figure in America to write an anti-slavery tract. My grandfather Rev, George Mair was the only student ever awarded a gold watch by Mt. Hermon School for never missing a class. My father George Fisk Mair rejected the notion that the purpose of being a college professor was for personal aggrandizement and research and publishing opportunities and remained a dedicated teacher all his life.

Uncle David and Aunt Patricia Mair stood up for the black community in Tennessee in the 1960s and the KKK burned a cross on their lawn. Ultimately, it is the values we each embrace personally and live by that matter I have come to believe.

The Problem with Capitalists and Republicans

The problem with capitalism is that the theory is that if you take a risk you reap the reward or the punishment of taking that risk. The reality seems to be if you are a member of today's privileged class and you take a risk you get bailed out if things go wrong, but if you are not a member of that privileged class you get punished for something you had nothing to do with.

Quakers are alarmed that Congress would respond to the problem of privileged people's flights being delayed because of the 911 sequester but do nothing to restore cuts to the Head Start, Low Income Fuel Assistance, or Housing subsidy programs for underprivileged people. Quakers are also alarmed that the deaths of three white people at the Boston Marathon receive a nation-wide response but the murders of 17 people of color in the next three months or the deaths of thousands of civilian men, women, and children in Iraq and Afghanistan at American hands hardly raise an eyebrow.

I promise I won't be so political in the rest of this book, but I guess all this stuff was fermenting in my mind since April 15, 2014 in Boston. AA and Al-anon teach people to accept life on life's terms and that is a philosophy that leads to a more serene life than political activism certainly.

I suppose this has always been true and some of our ancestors benefited in ways which allowed all of us to grow up relatively well off and educated and with a head start in life. Many of my ancestors were Republicans. Some people benefit from being born with higher intelligence or greater physical beauty, or family money. Life isn't fair and people are not born with equal opportunity, but we all have a choice on how we play the cards we are dealt.

I have had to overcome some rather severe difficulties and I also benefitted from my ancestors privileged lives. That's just the way it is.

Alex and her boyfriend broke up (amicably according to them). Alex was working two jobs in Newburyport at the Natural Grocer and the Port Tavern. I was promoted to Facilities Manager at the UU Church and had a new boss, Bill. We moved the church's data processing to the cloud, Microsoft 360 to be precise. I retired as Treasurer for the New England Quakers and became President of the Sons & Daughters of the First Settlers of Newbury.

Peru

Figure 96 Arequipa, Peru 2014

I spent two weeks in Peru in June. I loved it. Altitude sickness appeared to be a serious problem for several visitors, but I did not suffer from it. I enjoyed Lake Titicaca, and Colca Canyon, I really enjoyed the spiritual beauty of Machu Pichu and the scenic and historical beauty of Arequipa. I was disappointed by the line drawings on the desert at Nazca. The only way to see the line figures is by air, and most of the small airplanes the tourists fly circle too quickly to get a good look.

The Andes are quite spectacular. The high plains are dotted with alpacas, and llamas. I saw Andean condors at Colca Canyon and drank Inca Kola every day. Chewing cocoa leaves for altitude sickness didn't have any noticeable effect on me.

Newbury 2010s

On a typical Friday this year I would spend the morning picking melons at Arrowhead Farm, and I often had lunch at Anchor Pizza in Newburyport where everybody knows my name! I would work in the afternoon at the UU Church. I often would take a break for coffee at 3PM at Cafe di Sienna (now the Commune Café).

France

Figure 97 Carcassonne, France

The next year I spent two weeks in southern France. The medieval town of Carcassonne, the Arles of Van Gogh, and the town of Avignon were great places to visit! My travelling partner and I were a little taken aback by the crude bathroom facilities especially on major highway rest areas. The food, as one might expect, was excellent although I didn't choose to sample the abundant supply of wine.

Quakers

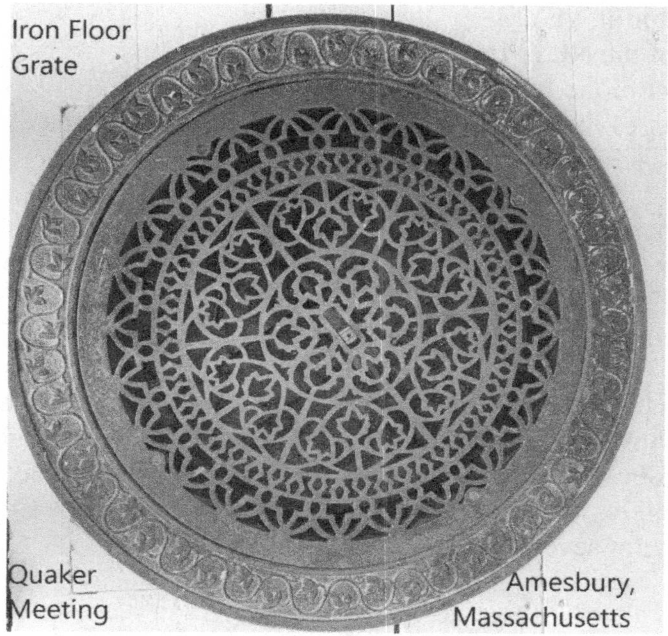

Figure 98 Iron Grate at Quaker Meeting House Amesbury, MA

The Quaker Religion, The Amesbury Friends Meeting, and the New England Yearly Meeting of the Religious Society of Friends have been an important part of my life. I have participated actively in this institution at both the local and regional level including serving as:

Clerk of the Amesbury Building Committee
Clerk of the Amesbury Finance Committee
Clerk of the Amesbury Meeting
Representative to the Amesbury Council of Churches
Archivist of the Amesbury Meeting

Member of the Salem Quarter Grants Committee
Treasurer of the Salem Quarter
Clerk of the Salem Quarter
Representative to the Massachusetts Council of Churches

Hartford and Quakers 2015-2017

Member of Permanent Board of NEYM
Treasurer of NEYM
Clerk of the NEYM Archives Committee
Member of the Legacy Grant Committee
Member of the Board of Managers of the Pooled Funds
Various ad hoc Committees

The Board of Managers (BoM) of the Pooled funds had bi-monthly lunches at the Harvard Club in Boston. The BoM has the duel and somewhat conflicting goals of socially responsible investing and producing investment income for local meetings.

Quakers worship in silence, have no priests, are often peace activists, and believe there is that of God in everyone (the inner light). Being a Quaker may lead to other activities. I, for example, have led Alternatives to Violence workshops at the Middleton Correctional Facility for several years.

Figure 99 View from Harvard Club Boston, MA

Honestly, I sometimes find the self-righteousness of Quakers somewhat obnoxious. The strange thing is that Quakers are usually right and ahead of their time on most important social issues!

Figure 101 Quaker Meeting House Amesbury, MA

Figure 100 Ed in Rome, Italy

Chapter XXVII Newbury, MA and Hartford, CT 2015

2015 was a particularly stressful year for me. In December of the previous year my sister Marggie had been diagnosed with a brain tumor, glioblastoma. She had surgery and was recovering from that at a nursing home where I spent Christmas with her and Mark and his husband at the nursing home.

I continued to work at the UU Church Monday through Thursday and drove to Hartford every weekend. I took Marggie out to lunch and to chemo at Hartford Hospital several times. Our cousins, Diane, Cindy, and Barb came up for Marggie's birthday in January. I was helped greatly during this time by Carolyn, Wes, Molly, and Patty. Marggie was also supported by the people from her church, St. James, in West Hartford and by classmates from her years at Smith College. The cat sitters came faithfully every day to feed Marggie's two cats, Nutmeg and Flip.

Towards the end Marggie had a live-in aide who really took very good care of her. I sometimes stayed at Marggie's house during her three stays at Hartford Hospital. On other weekends, my childhood friends, Howie and David, graciously offered me hospitality in Northampton and Amherst. Some weekends I stayed at the 1620 House in Simsbury, CT.

Italy

I went to Italy that summer while Marggie was very sick because she was not conscious much of the time and I didn't think she would want me to stop living my life. I visited Rome, Florence, Sienna, Pisa, Pompeii, and Assisi.

I stopped at home when I returned for 24 hours and then drove to Hartford. Marggie died the next morning and I will always be haunted by the image of the funeral home attendants putting her body into a bag and taking it away.

Figure 102 Tivoli, Italy

Figure 103 St. Teresa by Bernini Rome, Italy

The next couple of weeks are a blur. Somehow, I managed to arrange Marggie's funeral at St. James Episcopal Church in West Hartford, empty her condominium and arrange for the sale of it. My granddaughter Vera was born the day before Marggie's memorial service which was a blessing but sad because Alex and her husband could not come to the service and, except for my cousins, I had no family there to support me.

Patty took custody of Marggie's cats and my daughter's husband Steve prepared the condo for sale. The Assistant Pastor of the Church helped me donate Marggie's furniture to a charity. I gave the Hebrew books she was studying to a Synagogue, and gave her pictures and other books to relatives and her friends.

Apparently, she had made no provision in her will for a gravestone so I bought that for her.

Figure 104 Hartford, CT

Margaret Granville Mair (January 24, 1953 - July 13, 2015)

My sister was born in Princeton, NJ and died in West Hartford, CT. Like myself, she spent much of her early life in Northampton, MA where we both attended the Smith College Day School. She attended Smith College and later got MA degrees from Syracuse University in Library Science and from Trinity College in American Studies. She worked as a paralegal for attorneys, as a research assistant at the Mark Twain House and Harriet Beecher Stowe House, and as the archivist at the University of Hartford. She also ran her own archival consulting firm working with several insurance companies and non-profit organizations. Marggie never married, although she did have some romantic relationships. She was always very active with her church and

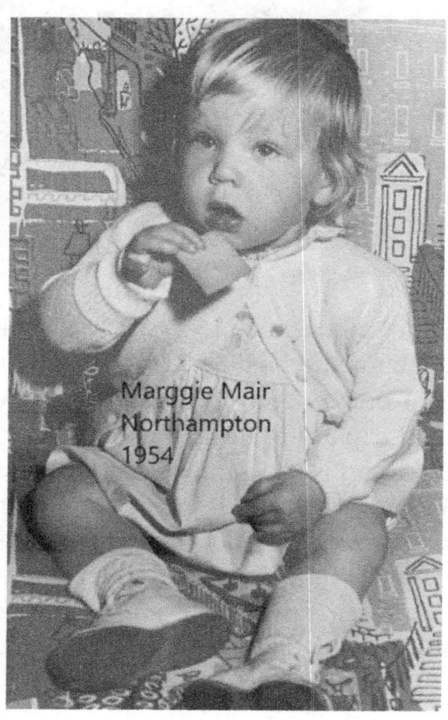

Figure 105 Margaret Mair as a baby

Figure 106 Ed, Marggie, and Uncle David in Marquette, Michigan

interested in local history and genealogy. She was an active member of the Wadsworth Athenaeum and Historical Wethersfield. Marggie and I had a falling out when our mother died but I think we worked it out during subsequent road trips to Michigan and to visit ancestral homes in New York, Vermont, and New Hampshire. She was always fond of my daughter Alex, and when she died, she left her entire estate to Alex, and her alma maters. She left only her personal possessions and car to me. This hurt my feelings but as I later discovered she had written her will in 1996 long before our falling out, and presumably because she assumed, she would outlive me which seems like a reasonable assumption.

Chapter XXVIII Hampstead NH and Newbury MA and Travels 2016 - 2017

My life since then has been somewhat like a dream. Aside from my daughter and grandchildren, my closest blood relatives are second cousins. I am the only survivor from my extended family.

I moved to my daughter's house in Hampstead, NH and rented my house on Plum Island. New Hampshire doesn't have any income tax or sales tax, but it does have high fees for car registrations and licenses as I found out when I transferred these documents to that state. I was happy to be in the same house with my daughter and granddaughter, but my daughter and son-in-law were not pleased to be starting their new family life with me around.

I was very active in a few 12 Step programs while I lived in Hampstead. As of 2019 I am still attending meetings there on Tuesdays and Thursdays. I moved out in early 2017 and back to Plum Island. This seems to be a better arrangement for everybody involved. However, I did have the experience of living in New Hampshire during the Presidential primary season and I made several good friends in Hampstead whom I still see often.

Figure 107 Ed at the wedding of Alex Mair and Steve Goss in 2015

France and Spain

In 2016 I went to Northeast Spain and Southeast France. I visited Monserrat, Barcelona, Andorra, Toulouse, Arles, Carcassonne, Marseilles, Nimes, Avignon, and Perpignan. I became quite interested in the Cathars of Carcassonne, called Albigensian heretics, by the Roman Catholic Church which tried to wipe them out during a crusade. Blue jeans (denim-de Nimes) were invented in Nimes. Perpignan in France was the capital of the Kingdom of Majorca. Which is now mostly in Spain. Half a bridge remains in Avignon. Van Gogh's yellow café and Roman ruins still exist in Arles.

Figure 108 Avignon, France

Bridge in Avignon, France

Romanesque Cathedral in Toulouse

Figure 109 Toulouse, France

In 2017 I visited Portugal and western Spain. I visited, Lima, Porto, Evora, Sintra, and Queluz in Portugal and Merida, Trujillo, and Plascencia in the Extremadura region of western Spain. Evora was an area dominated by Cork trees. Sintra was a city of fairy tale castles, and Extremadura was the harsh land of conquistadores and Roman ruins.

Red Sox and Patriots and Vermont

During the years 2007– 2017 I was a devoted sports fan. I attended several Red Sox games in Boston and watched the New England Patriots on TV almost every weekend. Since I often went to Stowe, Vermont on holiday weekends I recall watching several games at the Sunshine Bar in Stowe. Other Restaurants I liked in Stowe included the Dutch Pancake House and Cactus Pete's.

Although, I wasn't skiing during these years because of an old knee injury, I did visit the Stowe resort to drive to the top of Mt. Mansfield and came down the mountain on a slide. I also went through Smugglers notch a couple of times.

Figure 110 Stowe, VT

Margy and moving back to Plum Island

In late 2016 I ended one relationship and began another on "Our Time" a cyber-dating site for senior citizens. Margy and I emailed for a couple of months and finally decided to meet at a Denny's Restaurant in Salem, NH in January 2017. After dinner I offered Margy a rose and she accepted it.

Margy was living in Lexington and we went to the April commemorations of the battles of Lexington and Concord that began at dawn. We soon decided to move back to Plum Island together which worked out quite well as my tenants had moved out. So, I left New Hampshire and returned to Massachusetts.

I am confident that this relationship will last as we have similar interests and political views, and 12 Step experience. We have compatible religious views and we are not codependent! We successfully navigated the putting down of Margy's dog Chelsea and her cat Chloe. We often have grandchildren Jackson and Lana with us on weekends while their parents work. Margy's daughter Sarak is a frequent visitor.

Figure 111 Ed, Sarak, and Margy at home on Plum Island

Pennsylvania and the Delaware River

Figure 112 Delaware River

Kollner, Augustus, 1813-1906 - Artist. *Delaware River at Easton Pa.* Watercolors (Paintings). *Free Library of Philadelphia* https://libwww.freelibrary.org/digital/item/55744. (accessed Oct 11. 2019)

Ever since 2000, when I met my second cousin Diane Taggart and her father Bill at my Uncle Gerrish Thurber's memorial service, I have made a trip at least once a year to Pennsylvania to visit Diane, Cindy, and Barbara, three sisters who all live with their families in the Newtown, Bucks County area. In 2018 I made two trips, one to a family reunion and one to Bill Taggart's memorial service.

The sisters made trips to Hartford for my sister's last birthday and to her memorial service in Hartford, support I really appreciated. They and their families also attended Marggie's burial service in Ewing, NJ. I have watched football with them, celebrated the Fourth of July with them, and talked politics and religion with them.

The same year I attended Bill's service, Margy attended a relative's burial in the same cemetery! Even more of a coincidence after both services each of us attended a luncheon at the same restaurant, which in the last century was a farm owned by our Fisk ancestors!

When Margy and I travel we often take Margy's grandchildren Jackson and Lana. We took them on both trips to PA this past year and they really enjoyed swimming in our cousins' swimming pools.

It is a long drive but Margy's sister Mary lives in Easton, PA so we can visit relatives from both our families. We have been to the Crayola factory in Easton twice! I think the drive along the Delaware River and through the Delaware Water Gap is one of the prettiest drives in the United States. I often drive back that way although it makes for a considerably longer trip than taking the Interstate highways.

I very much enjoy spending time with my grandchildren, Vera and Ashton, and Margy's grandchildren, Lana, Jackson and Jayden. I also want to recognize Sarak's daughter Phoebe and Steve's son Brayden although I don't see them as much. That is my family during these autumn years of life.

I am reading a lot and then getting rid of the books as soon as I read them. Downsizing makes one realize how little value material stuff has at the end of life. I learned this lesson disposing of my father, mother, and sister's possessions which meant a lot to them but little to others still living.

Personal experience and genealogical research make one realize how little we can leave behind to those we love. This is one reason I decided to write this book.

Hawaii 2019

Margy and I went to Hawaii in April 2019. We visited with Margy's long lost stepdaughter Kathy Powell in Honolulu. We did the usual tourist things such as Waikiki, Diamond Head, The USS Arizona and volcanos. It was particularly distressing to see the Arizona memorial closed because necessary repair funds had been diverted to the southern border of the continental United States..

We left Oahu and visited three other islands: Maui, Kauai, and the big island of Hawaii. We enjoyed our visits to all three islands. It is the paradise one imagines. The people, the food, the beaches, and the flora and fauna are remarkable!

The takeover of Kauai by chickens, the sunsets on Hawaii, and the architecture of the hotels are very memorable.

Figure 113 Monkey Tree

Figure 114 Margy and Kathy at Hickam AFB

Margy and Kathy Powell at Hickam Military Base in Honolulu 2019.

Figure 115 Ed and Margy on Hawaii (Big Island)

Ed Mair and Margy Powell At Hawaii Hotel 2019.

Prep School Reunion at Williston-Northampton School – Easthampton, MA 2019

I will leave this story here. I hope there will be many more chapters to write! For the last year I have served with David Reichenbacher, Steve Trudel, Jim Moffit, Jim Fisher, and Bill Morrison on the 50th year reunion committee for the Class of 1969 at Williston-Northampton School. We had the opportunity to write and speak to many of our classmates during the year. My roommate Gary Baumer and 38 others joined us for the reunion which Margy and I thoroughly enjoyed.

Figure 116 Ed and Gary at Williston Easthampton, MA

Figure 117 Margy and her children

It was my privilege to help Jim Fisher conduct a memorial service for our departed classmates. I would like to give a last shout out to three of my best friends from Williston, Bill Goldman, Jim McNally, and Gary Mysorski, who have all passed away. Shortly after the reunion our friend Steve Trudel passed away. Bill Morrison, Dan Becker, Peter Clark and I attended a moving memorial service for Steve at the Unitarian Church in Northampton.

Figure 119 Ed looking at Vera

Figure 118 White Horse in Wiltshire, England 2006

Figure 121 Lana, Margy, and Jack at Hellcat Trail, Plum Island

Figure 120 Lana, Jaden, Jack. Sarah, Ed

Figure 123 Margy Moss Powell in Hawaii

Figure 122 Sheep in Avesbury, England

Figure 124 Windham ROMEO Club: Joe, Bob, Jim., Richard, Ed, Fred, Tom, John

INDEX

Hampstead, Vermont, travel, and return to Plum Island

Made in the USA
Coppell, TX
01 April 2021

52832895R00111